TEACHING
GONG YOGA

TEACHING GONG YOGA

THEORY AND PRACTICE

MEHTAB BENTON

Bookshelf Press

Teaching Gong Yoga: Theory and Practice
Copyright © 2014 by Michael Benton

All rights reserved. No part of this book may be used or reproduced by any means, graphic, electronic, or mechanical, including photocopying, recording, taping or by any information storage system without the written permission of the publisher except in the case of brief quotations embodied in critical articles and reviews.

Foreign publication rights available from the publisher.

Bookshelf Press books may be ordered by contacting:

Bookshelf Press
PO Box 50028
Austin, TX 78763
www.bookshelfpress.com
orders@bookshelfpress.com

You should not undertake any exercise or therapeutic regimen recommended in this book before consulting your personal physician. Neither the author nor the publisher shall be responsible or liable for any loss or damage allegedly arising as a consequence of your use or application of any information or suggestions contained in this book.

Cover and interior art by Brandi November Lyons (hari-and-avatar.com).

ISBN: 978-1-939239-09-9 (pbk)

Library of Congress Control Number: 2014908882
Printed in the United States of America

The mallet is the will of the infinite,

The gong, the creation,

And the sound is the spirit song,

The heartbeat of the soul.

Yogi Bhajan

Contents

Introduction   1

What Is Gong Yoga?   3

Gong Yoga: Five Levels of Existence   7
    The Yogic Model and the Gong
    The Koshas and the Practices of Yoga

The Yoga Teacher as Gong Player   11
    The Gong As Map of the Body
    The Gong Playing Areas
    The Gong: Rhythm and Volume
    The Gong: Basic Skills and Equipment

Asana and the Gong: Playing for the Physical Body   19
    Classification of Yoga Asanas
    Playing the Gong for Langhana and Brimhana
    Timing Asanas with the Gong
    Sun Salutations and the Gong
    Asana Sequences with the Gong
    Hatha Yoga Sequence with the Gong
    Vinyasa Flow Yoga Sequence with the Gong
    Kundalini Yoga Sequence with the Gong
    The Gong Yoga Teacher's Practice: Asana
    Asana Sequence for Playing the Gong

Pranayama and the Gong: Playing for the Energy Body   47
    Sound, Prana and the Five Tattvas
    The Energy Body and Yogic Anatomy
    The Five Vayus and the Gong
    The Three Major Nadis and the Gong
    The Seven Chakras and the Gong
    Playing the Gong for the Chakras
    The Energy Body and the Breath Cycle
    Pranayama Practices and the Gong
    The Gong Yoga Teacher's Practice: Pranayama

Mantra and the Gong: Playing for the Emotional Body   89
    The Gong, Mantras and the Science of Naad
    Nada Yoga and the Inner Sounds
    The Gong Yoga Teacher's Practice: Mantra

Meditation and the Gong: Playing for the Knowledge Body   99
    Yoga Techniques and Meditation
    Mudras and Gong Meditation
    Playing the Gong for Meditation
    The Gong Yoga Teacher's Practice: Meditation

Ritual and the Gong: Playing for the Bliss Body   117
    The Five Elements and Performance of Rituals
    The Gong Yoga Teacher's Practice: Ritual

Relaxation and the Gong: Playing for Integration   123
    Yoga Practices for Relaxation
    Playing the Gong for Relaxation
    Build and Release Cycles for Gong Relaxation
    The Gong and Yoga Nidra

The Gong and Styles of Yoga   143
    Kundalini Yoga and the Gong
    Hatha Yoga and the Gong
    Vinyasa Flow Yoga and the Gong
    Ashtanga Yoga and the Gong
    Restorative Yoga and the Gong
    Prenatal Yoga and the Gong
    Children's Yoga and the Gong
    Yoga for Seniors and the Gong

Guidelines for Teaching Gong Yoga   157
    Teaching and Playing the Gong
    Gong Maps and Playing Techniques
    The Structure of a Gong Yoga Class

Introduction

All yoga is based upon sound. The sound of the breath, the sound of a mantra, and even the unheard sounds realized only in the deepest state of meditation, all these sounds represent the essence of yoga, the vibrations and frequencies that take us from the gross to the subtle, from the finite to the infinite.

And of all the sounds, it is the Sound of the Gong that most closely represents what Yoga sounds like.

Within the Gong are all the sounds of the universe. Its holistic resonance brings us to a one-pointed centeredness, a welcomed integration of disparate consciousness into a single moment of wholeness where all possibilities exist. Its sound envelope creates a unified field of consciousness that is the purpose of all yoga practices.

And while Yoga can certainly be experienced without the Gong, why would you?

Yogi Bhajan the master of Kundalini Yoga who brought the Gong to the practice of yoga in the Western world said, "The sound of the Gong is the first sound in the universe, the sound that created this universe. It is the primal whisper of the soul, and its sound is the echo of the Original Word that created the world, the sound within all sounds."

For all of its power to enhance and accelerate the practices of yoga, the use of the Gong is often relegated to the end of the yoga class as a pleasant way to relax. Yet the gong can also be a powerful accompaniment to the practices of asana, pranayama, mantra, mudra and meditation, if the yoga teacher understands the theory and techniques of playing the gong in such a manner.

In my previous work, *Gong Yoga*, I expressed my hope that it would be seen as a pioneering effort to encourage the use of the gong in the practice of yoga. In this book, my intention is to show you how this can be done.

The Gong

is the first and last instrument

of the Human Mind.

Yogi Bhajan

What Is Gong Yoga?

Gong Yoga uses the sound of the Gong with the practices of Yoga to energize and facilitate the movement of prana to heal the body, clear the mind and elevate the consciousness. It is an integration of Nada Yoga (yoga of sound) and Laya Yoga (yoga of absorption) with the practices of Hatha Yoga and Kundalini Yoga.

The practice of Gong Yoga uses the techniques of asana, mudra, bandha, pranayama, and mantra to prepare the body and mind to optimally receive and interact with the sound of the gong so that an extended state of spontaneous meditation and therapeutic relaxation occurs.

Unlike other yoga disciplines that can be done as an individual practice, Gong Yoga requires a teacher to play the gong while the practice is done. It is best experienced when the yoga teacher is also a skilled gong player, and when the students can give themselves fully and freely to the sound of the gong.

Origins of Gong Yoga

The association of the sound of the gong and the practice of yoga is mentioned as early as the 14th century by Yogi Swatmarama in the *Hatha Yoga Pradipika*, one of the seminal works on the practice of hatha yoga.

In the final chapter of the *Pradipika* there is a discussion of the stages the yogi passes through on his journey to enlightenment. One of the distinguishing landmarks is the experience of hearing the internal sounds produced by the awakening of the Kundalini energy of awareness. These inner sounds progress in subtlety as awareness increases. The first stages of sound are heard as the sound of the ocean itself. From this roaring wave-like sound, the yogi then hears the sound of various drums that are refined into "the sound of the conch, the gong, and the horn." Indeed, another ancient text notes that when the Kundalini energy awakens the heart center, the listener experiences an internal silent sound like "a gong exploding at the center of the sun." Gradually the crashing sound of the gong dissolves until the yogi hears only a humming like that of the honeybee and becomes completely absorbed.

These inner sounds heard by the yogis in deep meditation, brought about by the inner practices of yoga such as pratyahara, dhyana, and dharana, were externalized by students and followers through instruments and music in a form of Nada Yoga that were then used in the external practices of yoga such as asana, mudra and pranayama.

Different regions of India favored particular instruments for their meditation practices, including flutes and drums, but it was in the areas of the world now known as Pakistan, Afghanistan, Tibet and northern India that the gong became the instrument of the yogi.

Gong Yoga in the Twentieth Century

The explicit use of the gong to facilitate yoga and meditation in modern times can be traced to Northern India in the late nineteenth century when Kundalini Yoga masters played the gongs to awaken the intuitive faculties and create a transcendent consciousness in themselves and their students. One such yoga master was Sant Hazara Singh, a great Sikh mystic and Kundalini yogi of the early twentieth century. Hazara Singh lived in Gujaranwala, India (which is now Pakistan) and in 1937, he accepted an 8-year old boy as his student and taught him Kundalini Yoga, Gatka (a sword-based martial art), and gong meditation.

In 1945, Hazara Singh pronounced the boy at the age of 16 to be a Kundalini Yoga master. Twenty-four years later in 1969, the boy, now a man by the name of Yogi Bhajan, was teaching Kundalini Yoga in the back of a furniture store in Los Angeles. Soon a community of hippies turned yogis were studying with the teacher who shared his knowledge of yoga, meditation, and the gong.

Yogi Bhajan originally introduced the gong in his yoga classes to rehabilitate the nervous systems of the young drug users now turned yoga students. By the 1970s and 1980s, the gong was turning up throughout the United States and around the world in the Kundalini Yoga ashrams he had inspired. In 1990 Yogi Bhajan taught an instructional class in how to play the gong that inspired a monograph a few years later by Gurucharan Singh Khalsa called *The Art of the Gong*. The first book to formalize the practice of yoga with the gong, *Gong Yoga*, was originally written in 1997 and published in 2008.

Gong Yoga Today

Along with the publication of *Gong Yoga*, the use of the gong in the practice of yoga grew beyond its almost exclusive use by Kundalini Yoga teachers as yoga teachers from other traditions experimented with the gong in their classes. Gong players also began adding yoga practices into their gong trainings and workshops, creating an innovative if highly varied approach to using the powerful sound of the gong with the transformational practices of yoga.

As with any emerging style of yoga, there is often experimentation and interpretation by the early practitioners and teachers that create a vital expression of the practice but sometimes at the expense of consistency, particular if the underlying structure of the practice is not explicitly understood.

And indeed, there is an underlying structure to practicing and teaching Gong Yoga that goes beyond simply playing the gong while yoga is done. This structure is based upon one of the oldest models in yoga, the concept of the five bodies of existence, the Panchamaya Koshas, and when this model is employed with specific gong playing techniques that complement the authentic yoga practices of asana, pranayama, mantra and meditation, then the full power of Gong Yoga, in both its theory and practice, can be realized.

By sustained practice

of all the components of yoga,

The impurities dwindle away,

And wisdom's radiant light shines forth

with discriminative knowledge.

Yoga Sutras (II:28)

Gong Yoga: Five Levels of Existence

The experience of practicing and teaching Gong Yoga is more easily understood by using one of the oldest contextual models that explains how yoga works. This model helps us appreciate the multi-level nature of yoga and its practices, as well as how various yoga techniques, when combined with the sound of the gong, take the practitioner of Gong Yoga through increasingly subtle layers of existence until the ultimate goal of yoga is reached, union and merger into the Infinite Self.

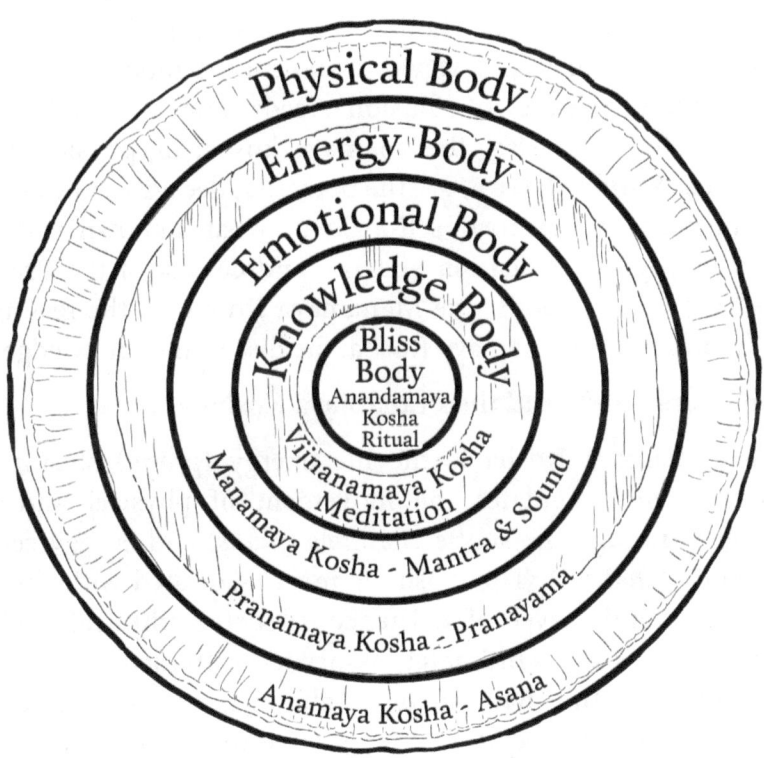

The Yogic Model and the Gong

The model that explains how the gong works in the practice of yoga first appears in one of the earliest yogic texts, the Taittiriya Upanishad (circa 6th century BCE) and is referred to as the Panchamaya Kosha model, or the five (*pancha*) layers (*koshas*) of the mutually coexisting energies of the human experience. The koshas are identified in the Upanishads, and later in the Advaita Vedenta, as five successive layers, or bodies, of objectification that hide the nature (*maya*) of the True Self (*atman*), much like wrappers that hide our eternal essence. Through the practice of yoga, we are able to pierce these veils of illusory separateness and achieve the realization of Oneness.

The Physical Body and the Anamaya Kosha

The outer wrapper, or first kosha, is called the Anamaya Kosha and represents the physical body, the most completely objectified representation of self. The word *ana* means food as this layer of existence, or sheath of illusion, feeds our strongest sense of individuated self. Also, the anamaya kosha, or physical body, is known as **Sthula Sharira**, or "the body that decays" without food.

The next three layers of self make up what is known as the subtle body in yoga, or **Sukshma Sharira**, and consist of the Pranamaya Kosha, or energy body, the Manamaya Kosha, or the feeling mind body, and the Vijnanamaya Kosha, the discerning knowledge body.

The Energy Body and the Pranamaya Kosha

The Pranamaya Kosha is the life energy (*prana*) sheath of our existence and regulates the movement of physical and mental energies through the subtle channels (*nadis*) and energy centers of the body (*chakras*). This kosha is most associated with the breath, the first subtle level of existence after the physical body. The Pranamaya Kosha is intimately associated with the Anamaya Kosha, just as the breath is with the physical body, and both are dependent on each other and coexist almost as a one-to-one mapping.

The Emotional Body and the Manamaya Kosha

The Manamaya Kosha, the third layer of existence, is the mental (*mana* means mind) or emotional body that holds the physical and pranic body together through the passage of time and organizes our sensory sensations and feelings. This is also the aspect of self that controls sequential thought process and a continuing sense of identity or individuation.

The Knowledge Body and the Vijnanamaya Kosha

The Vijnanamaya Kosha, the fourth layer of existence, is the knowledge (*vijnana*) body or higher discerning intelligence that contains wisdom and the witnessing consciousness that allows us to realize the eternal truths. This is the most refined layer of the **Sukshma Sharira**, or the subtle body, where the experience of ordinary existence through time and space ends.

The Bliss Body and the Anandamaya Kosha

The Ananadamaya Kosha, the final layer of existence that hides the True Self, makes up the causal body in yoga, or the **Karana Sharira**, that exists beyond time and space and is the deepest essence of our being. This kosha is also known as the bliss (*ananda*) body for it contains everlasting happiness, love, and ecstasy that transcends the limiting human experience and brings us to the state of union.

The primary purpose of yoga is to gain full awareness and control over these five bodies or layers of energy, ranging from the gross machinations of the physical body with muscles, organs, and senses to the increasingly subtle realms of prana, feelings, thoughts, and eventually pure light.

The Koshas and the Practices of Yoga

Through all the practices of yoga, from the gross to the subtle, the five koshas of the self are affected by various yogic techniques. Practicing **asanas**, or yoga postures, strengthen the physical body (anamaya kosha) while the practice of **pranayama** or breath control works on the pranic body (pranamaya kosha). The emotional body (manamaya kosha) that processes our mundane thoughts and feelings is accessed through **mantra** and sacred sound. The knowledge body (vijnanamaya kosha) is essentially affected through **meditation** and practices such as mudras that direct prana to the highest centers. The bliss body (anandamaya kosha) is experienced through **ritual** and a transcendent state of relaxation and integration that dissolves the illusion (maya) of all five koshas.

For each kosha, and the yoga techniques that accompany them, one can trace the effects that the sound of the gong produces. When used with asana, pranayama, mantra, sound, meditation, ritual and relaxation, the gong accelerates the progress of the yogi in integrating the five koshas that make up the human experience and enables us to realize our eternal nature.

Understanding how the gong can be played with the various techniques of yoga to affect the physical, subtle and causal body is first step of our journey in practicing and teaching Gong Yoga.

The Yoga Teacher as Gong Player

All yoga is fundamentally about cultivating, storing, directing, and transforming prana, the vital life force energy of the universe that is instrumental in the elevation of consciousness. All asana, pranayama, mantra, mudra, bandha, and meditation are essentially about controlling and maximizing the flow of prana through the physical and subtle bodies in order to reconnect to the causal body, the eternal soul within each individuated consciousness, or *atman*.

With the usual practices of yoga, this prana is under the control of the individual practitioner and the role of the teacher is to instruct, guide and inspire the student to use the techniques of yoga in the most effective way to access and use this prana.

In the practice of Gong Yoga, the gong itself is an instrument of prana in that its sound both creates and directs the flow of the prana in the listener and practitioner. As such, the gong becomes the intermediary between the yoga teacher and the student and provides a method by which the teacher can support and guide the student in the utilization of the prana or vital life force that yoga works with.

To do this, the yoga teacher must attain a degree of skill in playing the gong before teaching Gong Yoga. This skill requires familiarity with gong playing techniques, as well as understanding the unique requirements of playing the gong while teaching yoga. More importantly, this skill also requires that the gong player or yoga teacher understand the basic nature, instrumentality and methodology of using the gong to affect the yoga practice.

In essence, the yoga teacher needs a familiarity of how the gong moves prana through different playing techniques and the various playing areas of the gong. We need to see the gong not only as a tool in the practice of yoga but also as a **map** to access the physical, emotional, and energy bodies of the practitioner.

The Gong As Map of the Body

The practice of yoga begins with the physical body as we move from the gross to the subtle through a refinement of practices and consciousness. The Gong itself can be used as a map of the physical body, and by playing various areas of the gong, the teacher can aid in directing prana to different regions of the body.

Body Map and the Gong

Ancient Indian philosophy, and many Western wisdom traditions, has as fundamental principle that the human body is the microcosm of the Universe, or the greater macrocosm. The principle that the divine is present in every object, cell and atom is the basis of many esoteric teachings and was popularized by the Hermetic writers during the Western renaissance with the phrases, "As above, so below,' and "As without, so within." This divine immanence means that the physical body itself is a map of the universal body, the One.

In Yoga, we see this principle illumined even in the name of Hatha Yoga that literally means Sun-Moon, a reference to the Sun energy and the Moon energy that exists both without and within the body. The third eye, for example, is where this Sun and Moon energy unite to bring enlightenment to the yoga practitioner. The spine, the central energy channel of the body in yoga where the Kundalini energy is channeled, is referred to in yogic texts as Meru-dandu, a reference to Mount Meru, a mountain considered to be the axis of the earth, and the energy channels (*nadis*) in the body are referred to as rivers while the five basic yogic energies of the body (*vayus*) are called winds. And in all evolutionary processes, there is an understanding that evolution proceeds from the bottom to the top, much like the Kundalini energy rises in the body from the base of the body up to the crown.

In a similar manner, the gong can provide a bridge between cosmology and biology when it is used as a map of the physical body. To do this, consider the gong as a representation of the human body. At the bottom of the gong is the base of the body, from the feet to the tip of the spine. At the top of the gong is the top of the body, the head and crown. In the center of the gong, or its heart, is the heart of the human body.

When the gong is played in the lower area, the lower areas of the body are affected. When the gong is played in the upper area, the organs and glands in the upper body are affected.

Furthermore when the gong is played with a downward movement, it corresponds to a downward movement of the body, and a similar correspondence for upward movements. By visualizing the human body superimposed over the gong face, the gong teacher can use different playing areas of the gong to direct the movement of prana through the body of the practitioner.

The Gong Playing Areas

From the discussion of the Gong as a map of the human body, we gain an appreciation of how different playing areas of the gong can be used by the Gong Yoga teacher. The nature, quality and the effect of the sound produced by the gong depend upon where the gong is struck or played.

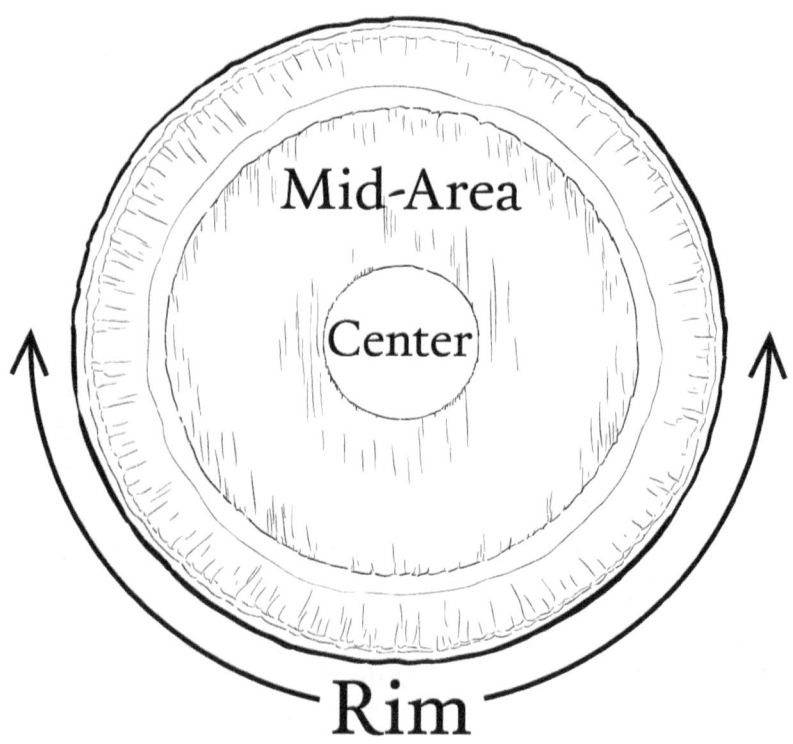

The Three Major Areas

The surface of the gong may be divided into three striking areas: Center area, Mid-area, and Rim area. On some gongs, you can see these areas clearly delimited by the finish on the surface. The center area appears to be like a small sun with a diameter about one-quarter the size of the entire gong. The rim area is slightly rough and extends in a few inches from the edge. The mid-area between the rim and the center is the largest playing area, sometimes colored between the darker rim and the brighter center. Each playing area produces a different quality of sound when struck.

Striking the gong near the center area gives a rich, enduring and carrying sound–almost like a strong fundamental note. Striking in the mid-area between the center and rim produces a deep, complete and swelling sound–rich and complex in tone coloring. Striking in the rim area gives an airy, sparkling and roaring sound–partial tones that transcend any specific pitch.

The Percussion Points

In addition to the three major areas, there are 14 discrete playing areas on the gong called percussion points. Think of the gong as a clock face divided into 12 areas, one for each hour. The 12 o'clock position is at the top of the gong (or more precisely in the top of the mid-area of the gong below the rim). The 6 o'clock position is at the bottom, again above the rim area. The other clock positions go around the outer mid-area of gong so there are 12 points or localized areas that can be struck. In the middle of the gong, there is a zero position so that the upper center area (before the mid-area begins) is known as "Up 0" and the lower center area is known as "Down 0." So we now have 14 total percussion points on the gong (including the two center "0" points) where the vast majority of the mallet strikes will occur.

Each percussion point produces a distinctive sound, and can be played in various sequences with other points to create a specific effect. For example, playing the percussion points 3, 6, 9, and 12 in repeated sequences distribute energy equally around the body.

The Gong: Rhythm and Volume

In addition to the playing areas of the gong, the Gong Yoga teacher uses the techniques of rhythm and volume to create, cultivate, and direct the prana during a yoga practice. The effects of increasing or decreasing the rhythm and volume when playing the gong are discussed in the sections on the various yoga techniques (asanas, pranayamas, etc.). In general, a faster rhythm or louder volume increases the movement of prana while a slower rhythm or softer volume consolidates the movement of prana. The playing areas struck and the intention of the player further modifies the effects of the rhythm and volume.

The Gong Basic Skills and Equipment

The book assumes that the yoga teacher has acquired a basic level of playing skills as outlined in the book *Gong Yoga* or the DVD course, *How To Play the Gong*. There should be familiarity with the playing areas, mallet strikes, and creating sequences of sound through playing the percussion points. While the gong itself is a good teacher and intuitive playing does develop through your own yoga practice and playing practice, familiarity with the basic playing techniques is essential to teach Gong Yoga. If you do not have the basic playing skills yet, then an experienced gong player can accompany you as you teach until you do so.

In addition to playing skills, a suitable gong is also required to teach gong yoga. While passionate arguments can be made for different sizes, types, and brands of gong, there are general guidelines that may be helpful.

First, the gong must be a suitable size to create a sound that can have a significant effect on the practitioner. If undersized, the gong will have more of a musical than a pranic impact. If oversized, the gong can overwhelm the practice and the practitioner. Personal opinions and experiences vary widely, but in general a preferred gong size for a Gong Yoga class is between 24 inches and 38 inches. A 30 to 34 inch gong is highly recommended for versatility.

There are roughly two major categories of gongs: Symphonic Gongs and Tuned Gongs. While the tuned gongs (such as the Planetary Gongs tuned to orbital frequencies) produce beautiful sounds and have a potent uniqueness, their limited range is best used for specific purposes. The symphonic gongs produce complex overtones and a strong fundamental note that give a wider range of playing options, especially for meditation and relaxation. Every Gong Yoga teacher should have at least one symphonic gong and may add tuned gongs as desired.

As far as manufacturing brands go, this is what gong players argue about! If you can play them or hear them played, that is the best way to select your gong.

Gong Equipment for the Gong Yoga Teacher

Here is a suggested list of the equipment needed to teach Gong Yoga, from basics to more advanced teaching.

Basic Set

- Gong – 24 inch to 36-inch Symphonic Gong
- Mallet – One mallet, sized appropriately for the gong
- Stand – Portable floor stand for playing while sitting

Intermediate Set

- Gongs – 30 inch to 36-inch Symphonic Gong
    Smaller Symphonic Gong or Tuned Gong
- Mallets – Two mallets, sized appropriately for both gongs
    One mallet the next size smaller.
- Stands – Portable floor stand
    Large upright stand for playing while standing

Advanced Set

- Gongs – 30 inch to 36-inch Symphonic Gong
    Smaller (or larger) Symphonic Gong
    Hand-held Gong
    Tuned Gongs, one or more
- Mallets – Mallets, sized appropriately for each gong
    Smaller pair(s) of mallets
    Rubbing mallet(s)
- Stands – Portable floor stand
    Large upright stand for playing while standing
    Stand for multiple gongs

Asana and the Gong: Playing for the Physical Body

The asanas, or postures, of yoga work directly on the physical body to improve muscular and skeletal functioning and benefit the organs and glandular system. In yoga philosophy, the physical body is akin to the Anamaya Kosha, or the sheath or level of existence that requires the taking of food to exist in the incarnated realm. It is the grossest level of existence, and it is most readily accessed through the technique of asana.

The gong affects the anamaya kosha, or physical body, in several ways. First, the gong produces a sound wave that is almost tangible, which stimulates the physical body by influencing the surface of the skin. The sonic touch of the gong can be a healing touch as its sound stimulates the body's dermatomes.

Dermatomes are surface areas of skin extending from the spine throughout the body. Through a network of nerves, these skin areas are connected to different organs in the body and with corresponding segments of the spinal cord. These skin areas can be stimulated by sound waves, much like a massage, and produce effects on corresponding organs and other areas of the body.

Secondly, when used with asanas, the sonic massage of the gong and its stimulation of the dermatomes bring additional benefits to the yoga practitioner, particularly in the area of pain relief. The sound of the gong has been found to be helpful in reducing pain associated with neck pain, headaches, cramping, muscle strains, and neurological pain (see *Gong Yoga: Healing and Enlightenment Through Sound*).

On a more subtle level, the sound of the gong has proven to be an excellent way to deepen the focus of the asana practitioner, allowing a deeper connection to the flow of energy or prana that is produced and released through the asana practice. On a practical level, the gong can be used to orchestrate and direct the movement of the yoga practitioner through the sequences of an asana practice.

Classification of Yoga Asanas

Most yoga practices in the Western world are based on the postures, or asanas, of Hatha Yoga and are a good introduction to understanding how the gong can be used in the practice and teaching of yoga.

The origins of the classical asanas in Hatha Yoga are shrouded in mystery and myth, going back to the god Shiva who is said to initially have taught 8,400,000 postures representing the 8,400,000 life forms the soul travels through to achieve enlightenment. (Depending upon interpretations, this number has also been represented as 840,000 and 84,000). Of these, 84 asanas were said to be primary in covering all aspects of the human existence.

Even so, there are still hundreds of asanas commonly taught in yoga. By putting them in general categories, we can more easily interact with the different types of postures, regardless of the specific asana, through the sound of the gong.

A classical approach to categorizing asanas is borrowed from the Vedic science of Ayurveda that uses yoga postures for healing and therapy. Asanas are primarily classified as being Brimhana or Langhana in nature by the effects they have on the body.

Langhana Asanas	Brimhana Asanas
Cool	Warm
Relax	Activate
Release energy	Build energy
Promote elimination	Promote strengthening
Aid parasympathetic nervous system	Aid sympathetic nervous system
Increase sensory activity	Increase motor activity
Aid in treatment of tension, stress, insomnia, constipation, headaches, chronic pain, irritability, arthritis, stroke, allergies, inflammation.	Aid in treatment of fatigue, low vitality, lethargy, diarrhea, poor circulation, depression, asthma, chronic fatigue, apathy, weakness.

When we use the traditional categorization of asanas according to body position or movement, we can create the following chart that relates the asana category to its ability to producing a Langhana or Brimhana effect, with the strongest producing Langhana and Brimhana asanas at the top of the chart and least producing at the bottom of the chart, as follows:

Langhana Asana Categories	Brimhana Asana Categories
Supine	Handstands, Arm Balances
Sitting	Back Bend
Twisting	Abdominal
Forward Bend	Standing
Inversions	Inversions

The supine postures are the most Langhana in nature, with the sitting postures next, followed by the twisting asanas and then the forward bending asanas. Handstands and arm balancing asanas produce the strongest Brimhana effect, followed in descending order by back bends, abdominal and finally standing postures. Notice that inversions (such as headstand and shoulderstand) have an equal effect of producing Langhana and Brimhana energy and are balancing in effect.

Playing the Gong for Langhana and Brimhana

The gong player can also create Langhana and Brimhana effects by controlling the rhythm, modulating the volume, or by striking different playing areas of the gong. In this way, the Gong Yoga teacher can enhance the effects that the various asanas have on the practitioner. In the simplest application, the gong can be played in a Langhana manner when Langhana postures are done and in a Brimhana manner when Brimhana postures are done.

How Gong Rhythm Affects Asana

As the rhythm, or rate, of striking the gong increases, the quality of Brimhana also increases. Similarly as the rhythm is slowed, the quality of Langhana increases. This would mean that for supine postures (Langhana), the gong is played slowly and for handstands the gong is played rapidly (Brimhana).

The rhythm ranges from slow to fast (using the baseline tempo of the individual gong player) according to the type of asana performed. Notice a moderate and equal rhythm corresponds to the inverted postures as they create a balance between Langhana and Brimhana.

Asana Categories	Rhythm Rate
Supine	Very Slow
Sitting	Slow
Twisting	Somewhat Slow
Forward Bend	Slightly slow
Inversions	Moderate equal rhythm
Standing	Slightly fast
Abdominal	Somewhat Fast
Back Bend	Fast
Handstands, Arm Balances	Very fast

The gong player also has the ability to moderate the effects of a Langhana or Brimhana asana by playing in contrast. For example, the Gong Yoga teacher can modify the Brimhana effects of a back bending posture by playing the gong slowly. Such an approach may be useful to create a specific response in the yoga practitioner, as for example when it is desired to cool or slow down a practice as a back bend is performed.

How Gong Volume Affects Asana

As the volume or intensity of striking the gong increases, the Brimhana quality also increases. Conversely, as the volume decreases, the quality of Langhana increases. For example, for supine postures the gong is played softly and for handstands the gong is played loudly.

The volume ranges from soft to loud according to the type of asana performed. Notice that a moderate volume (balanced) corresponds to the inverted postures that are balancing in effect.

Asana Categories	Volume Level
Supine	Very Soft
Sitting	Soft
Twisting	Somewhat Soft
Forward Bend	Slightly soft
Inversions	Moderate volume
Standing	Slightly loud
Abdominal	Somewhat loud
Back Bend	Loud
Handstands, Arm Balances	Very loud

As with rhythm, the gong player has the ability to moderate the effects of an asana by playing in contrast, such as playing softly for a back bend in order to reduce a tendency to over extend the posture.

Rhythm and Volume for Transitions and Sequencing

As students move from asana to asana, rhythm and volume can be combined to sequence the flow of energy and to set expectations for transitions between one group of postures and the next. Here are general guidelines to follow:

When moving from a posture that increases Brimhana, keep the

volume the same but **increase the rhythm**, such as:.
- Forward Bend to Back Bend – Volume remains slightly soft but rhythm gradually increases from moderately slow to fast.
- Sitting Posture to Standing Posture – Volume remains soft but rhythm gradually increases from slow to slightly fast.

When moving from a posture that increases Langhana, keep the rhythm the same but **decrease the volume**, such as:.
- Back Bend to Forward Bend – Rhythm remains fast but volume gradually decreases from loud to slightly soft.
- Standing Posture to Sitting Posture – Rhythm remains slightly fast but volume decreases from slightly loud to soft.

Once the transition occurs, volume and rhythm can be matched appropriately to the asana being performed. Notice that rhythm and volume are relative according to the individual's own playing style.

How Gong Playing Areas Affects Asana

The gong player can also increase or decrease the Langhana and Brimhana effects of an asana by striking different areas of the gong. Here are general guidelines for each category of asana:

Asana Categories	Gong Playing Area(s)
Supine	Bottom of gong; Side closest to player
Sitting	Near bottom of gong; Side closest to player
Twisting	Bottom mid-area; Middle from player
Forward Bend	Below center; Side farthest from player
Inversions	Alternate above and below center
Standing	Above center; Side closest to player
Abdominal	Top mid-area of gong; Middle from player
Back Bend	Near top of gong; Side farthest from player
Handstands, Arm Balances	Top of gong; Side farthest from player

Rhythm and volume may be integrated into these playing areas of the gong to maximize or moderate the Langhana and Brimhana effects of the asanas. For example, for a challenging arm balance, such as Scorpion pose, the gong can be played loudly and quickly at the top of the gong. For a handstand that is supported against the wall (and requires less effort), the gong can be played slower or softer at the top of the gong. Both asanas are high in Brimhana, yet the experience of the practitioner is different in the execution of the two postures. This difference in the effort required by the postures can be acknowledged by moderating the volume and rhythm.

Langhana and Brimhana Playing in Summary

While you may create various combinations of rhythm, volume and playing areas to match the Langhana and Brimhana qualities of various asanas, here are general guidelines for these playing techniques:

1. Faster rhythm supports Brimhana. Slower rhythm supports Langhana.
2. Louder volume supports Brimhana. Softer volume supports Langhana.
3. Playing upper half of the gong supports Brimhana. Playing lower half of the gong supports Langhana.
4. Playing the area farthest from the player supports Brimhana. Playing the area closest to the player supports Langhana.

Timing Asanas with the Gong

Asanas are typically held for a number of breaths, a number of repetitions, or for a prescribed length of time. The gong can serve as a timer or counter when working with asanas by creating a signal to move into or release from one posture to the next.

For example, in the practice of Ashtanga yoga the practitioner often holds a posture for a count of five or five breaths. The gong in this case may be struck rhythmically five times to signal the holding period for the asana. After the fifth gong strike, the practitioner moves into the next asana in the sequence and continues. In this way, an Ashtanga class could be conducted without words by using the gong to direct the flow of the class if the practitioner knows the prescribed sequence.

Alternatively, the gong can be struck only at the end of the holding period of an asana, signifying a time to release and move into the next posture. When the gong is struck, the practitioner inhales and then releases the posture on the exhale.

If the practitioner can hold a posture for an extended period of time, the gong can be played in various ways to release blocked energy and move prana along the energy lines of the asana, such as increasing the rhythm and the volume as the posture is held.

Teaching Considerations in Using the Gong with Asanas

If the asana practice requires much verbal instruction or visual demonstration, it may be necessary to have both a yoga teacher and a gong player working together. The gong player will have to be aware of creating space for verbal instructions by occasionally muffling or quieting the gong so the teacher can be heard.

As a posture is held, the gong may be played appropriately to enhance the energy of the asana. For example, an extended warrior pose could be accompanied by a steady almost martial tempo that is fiery and focused. A long forward bend, on the other hand, would be enhanced by a slow, watery beat that encourages release and letting go.

Again, the player must be skillful and cognizant of the asana practice itself to understand what is needed from the gong. Simply playing the gong while asanas are being done is not enough to make it an appropriate yogic tool.

In general, these guidelines may be followed when playing the gong with asanas:

- Upward moving postures receive upward strikes of the gong.
- Downward moving postures receive downward strikes of the gong.
- Centering or neutral movements receive strikes near the center of the gong.
- Challenging postures receive faster strikes. Releasing postures receive slower strikes.

Sun Salutations and the Gong

The most common Hatha asana practice is the classical Sun Salutation (Surya Namaskara). While there are many versions of Sun Salutations, modified by teachers over the last 100 years to suit their particular practice or lineage, the classical version consists of 12 postures or positions:

1. Pranamasana (Prayer pose)
2. Hasta Utthanasana (Raised arm pose)
3. Padahastasana (Hand to foot pose)
4. Ashwa Sanchalanasana (Equestrian pose)
5. Parvatasana (Mountain pose; also Downward Dog)
6. Ashtanga Namaskara (Eight Point Bowing; also Plank)
7. Bhujangasana (Cobra pose; also Upward Dog)
8. Parvatasana (Mountain pose; also Downward Dog)
9. Ashwa Sanchalanasana (Equestrian pose)
10. Padahastasana (Hand to foot pose)
11. Hasta Utthanasana (Raised arm pose)
12. Pranamasana (Prayer pose)

These 12 positions are practiced twice to complete one round, changing sides (right leg, left leg) during Ashwa Sanchalanasana.

While there are variations (Upward Dog instead of Cobra, or Plank Pose instead of Eight Point Bowing), the general orientation (forward bend, backbend) of the sun salutation is fairly consistent.

A simple way to use the gong with sun salutations is to play one stroke of the gong for each posture. The rhythm of the strokes is equal, and may be slowed or increased depending upon how fast the sun salutation is to be done. While there are many ways to play these strokes, here is one simple and intuitive approach:

The postures in the salutation that have an upward movement or backbend take an upward strike on the top half of the gong. Postures that move downward or forward receive a downward strike on the bottom half of the gong. Postures that are centering or neutral in nature receive a strike near the center of the gong. Here are the gong strikes associated with the 12 asanas or postures that comprise a sun salutation:

Sun Salutation Asana	Gong Playing Technique
Pranamasana (Prayer pose)	Center Strike
Hasta Utthanasana (Raised arm pose)	Upward Strike
Padahastasana (Hand to foot pose)	Downward Strike
Ashwa Sanchalanasana (Equestrian pose)	Upward Strike
Parvatasana (Mountain pose; also Downward Dog)	Downward Strike
Ashtanga Namaskara (8-Point Bowing; or Plank)	Center Strike
Bhujangasana (Cobra pose; also Upward Dog)	Upward Strike
Parvatasana (Mountain pose; also Downward Dog)	Downward Strike
Ashwa Sanchalanasana (Equestrian pose)	Upward Strike
Padahastasana (Hand to foot pose)	Downward Strike
Hasta Utthanasana (Raised arm pose)	Upward Strike
Pranamasana (Prayer pose)	Center Strike

Surya Namaskara

Asana Sequences with the Gong

The following asana sequences from different styles of yoga may be practiced with the gong according to the movement and nature of each posture. The asana sequence is first given and then a way of playing the gong is specified for each posture.

Note that the gong does not need to be played with every posture in a sequence, and the gong playing guidelines may be adjusted as needed by the teacher.

Hatha Yoga Sequence with the Gong

The following sequence takes 35 to 50 minutes and is a beginner-friendly approach to a Hatha-based asana practice using the gong.

1. Sukhasana (Easy Pose)
2. Adho Mukha Svanasana (Downward Dog)
3. Surya Namaskar: (Sun Salutations)
4. Vrksasana (Tree)
5. Utthita Trikonasana (Extended Triangle)
6. Utthita Parsvakonasana (Extended Side Angle)
7. Dandasana (Staff)
8. Paschimottanasana (Seated Forward Bend)
9. Baddha Konasana (Bound Angle)
10. Upavistha Konasana (Wide Angle)
11. Navasana (Boat)
12. Salabhasana (Locust)
13. Setu Bandha Sarvangasana (Supported Bridge)
14. Viparita Karani (Half Shoulderstand or Legs-Up-the-Wall)
15. Supta Matsyendrasana (Reclining Twist)
16. Savasana (Corpse)

Suggested Gong Techniques for Hatha Yoga Sequence

Asana	Gong Playing Technique(s)
Sukhasana (Easy Pose)	Three slow medium-soft strikes near center
Adho Mukha Svanasana (Downward Dog)	Three slow medium-soft strikes, downward bottom half of gong
Surya Namaskar (Sun Salutation)	Same as previously described for 2-4 complete rounds
Vrksasana (Tree)	Three to five medium strikes, slightly below top rim
Utthita Trikonasana (Extended Triangle)	Strike diagonally, medium rhythm and volume each side
Utthita Parsvakonasana (Extended Side Angle)	Strike diagonally, increased rhythm and volume each side
Dandasana (Staff)	Three slow medium-soft strikes, downward bottom half of gong
Paschimottanasana (Seated Forward Bend)	Three slow soft strikes, downward bottom half of gong
Baddha Konasana (Bound Angle)	Three medium strikes, downward bottom half of gong
Upavistha Konasana (Wide Angle)	Three medium-loud downward strikes, bottom half of gong
Navasana (Boat)	Fast loud strikes right below center of gong
Salabhasana (Locust)	Medium fast and medium loud upward strikes top half of gong
Setu Bandha Sarvangasana (Supported Bridge)	Fast and medium loud upward strikes top half of gong
Viparita Karani (Supported Half Shoulderstand)	Alternate soft to medium slow strikes above and below center
Supta Matsyendrasana (Reclining Twist)	Medium to medium fast and medium loud bottom mid area
Savasana (Corpse)	As desired for relaxation

Vinyasa Flow Yoga Sequence with the Gong

The following sequence moves with the breath and incorporates vinyasa transitions between the postures on both sides while using the gong.

1. Tadasana (Mountain)
2. Surya Namaskar (Sun Salutations): 5 Rounds
3. Adho Mukha Svanasana (Downward Dog): 10 Breaths
4. Vinyasa to Virabhadrasana I (Warrior 1), right and left: 5 Rounds, 5 Breaths
5. Vinyasa to Virabhadrasana II (Warrior 2), right and left: 5 Rounds, 5 Breaths
6. Vinyasa to Virabhadrasana III (Warrior 3), right and left side: 5 Rounds, 5 breaths
7. Vrksasana (Tree), right and left: 5 Breaths
8. Natarajasana (Dancer), right and left: 5 Breaths
9. Garudasana (Eagle), right and left: 5 Breaths
10. Tadasana (Mountain)

The vinyasa transitions may be orchestrated by using the gong to signal the movement with the breath.

Suggested Gong Techniques for Vinyasa Flow Sequence

Asana	Gong Playing Technique(s)
Tadasana (Mountain) 5 breaths	Five slow medium-soft strikes near center
Surya Namaskar (Sun Salutations)	Same as previously described for five complete rounds
Adho Mukha Svanasana (Downward Dog) 10 breaths	Ten slow medium-soft strikes, downward bottom
Virabhadrasana I (Warrior 1) 5 breaths each side, 5 rounds	Above center, medium to fast, medium to loud
Virabhadrasana II (Warrior 2) 5 breaths each side, 5 rounds	Above center, fast, loud
Virabhadrasana III (Warrior 3) 5 breaths each side, 5 rounds	Above center, faster and louder
Vrksasana (Tree) 5 breaths each side	Medium strikes, slightly below top rim
Natarajasana (Dancer) 5 breaths each side	Medium-soft slower strikes, alternate above below center
Garudasana (Eagle) 5 breaths each side	Harder strikes, alternate above below center
Tadasana (Mountain) 10 breaths	Ten slow soft strikes near center

Kundalini Yoga Sequence with the Gong

Kundalini Yoga as taught by Yogi Bhajan is practiced in **kriyas**, or formalized sequences of postures, breathing techniques, mudras, meditations and mantras that are not altered or changed by the teacher except for modifying the length of time the exercise is done. While most Kundalini kriyas do not specify the explicit use of the gong for an exercise, the gong can be played with them, much in the same way that Kundalini music or mantras are used to accompany a kriya.

The following sequence of Kundalini postures (indicated by English names first, in keeping with the protocol of Kundalini Yoga) has been called the Magnificent Seven asanas for women to practice. Notice that the Breath of Fire (Agni Pran), the signature breath of Kundalini Yoga, is used with the second posture.

1. Cat Stretch, Knee Drops, or the Reclining Twist (Supta Matsyendrasana)
2. Stretch Pose (Uttanapadasana)
3. Cobra Pose (Bhujangasana)
4. Cat/Cow (Marjariasana)
5. Seated Forward Bend (Paschimottanasana)
6. Reclining Rock Pose (Supta Virasana)
7. Half-Shoulderstand (Ardha Sarvangasana; Vipariti Karani)
8. Corpse (Savasana)

Suggested Gong Techniques for Kundalini Sequence

Asana	Gong Playing Technique(s)
Cat Stretch or Reclining Twist (Supta Matsyendrasana) 5 times each side	Slow medium-soft strike for each movement, 5 rounds
Stretch Pose (Uttanapadasana) with Breath of Fire (Agni Pran) 1 minute	Fast, medium-loud below center
Cobra Pose (Bhujangasana) with Breath of Fire (Agni Pran) 1 minute	Fast, loud near top
Cat/Cow (Marjariasana) 3 minutes	Medium strike, above and below center on inhale/exhale
Seated Forward Bend (Paschimottanasana) 3 minutes	Soft, slow bottom half
Reclining Rock Pose (Supta Virasana)	Soft-medium, slightly faster bottom half
Half-Shoulderstand (Ardha Sarvangasana or Vipariti Karani)	Soft to medium slow strikes alternate above/below center
Savasana (Corpse)	As desired for relaxation

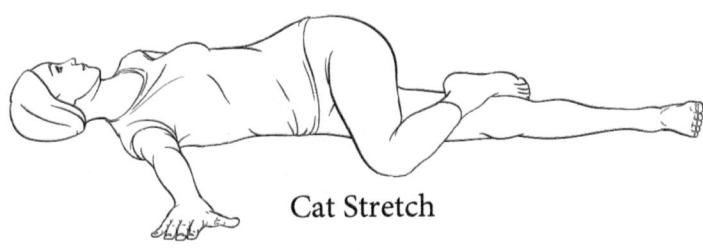
Cat Stretch

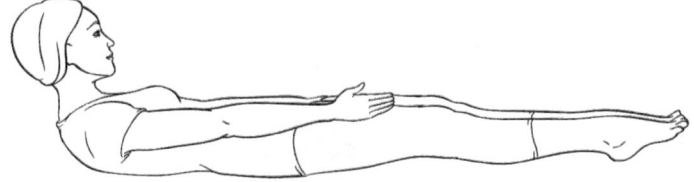
Stretch Pose

Cobra Pose

Cat/Cow

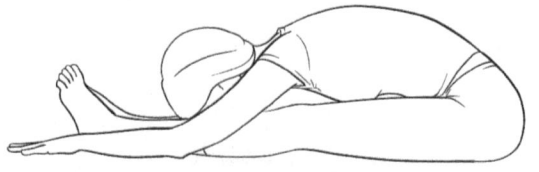

Seated Forward Bend

Reclining Rock Pose

Half-Shoulderstand

Corpse Pose

The Gong Yoga Teacher's Practice: Asana

The Gong Yoga teacher also practices asana when playing the gong by following the directive given by the sage Patanjali in the *Yoga Sutras* (2:46): "Asana is performed with steadiness and ease." When playing the gong, the teacher assumes a position and posture in relation to the gong that is stable and relaxed that allows the sound to be fully produced.

If the gong is played while sitting on the floor, the gong teacher may use any major seated asana, such as Sukhasana (Easy Pose) or Padmasana (Lotus Pose). One of the most effective seated asanas for playing the gong is on the heels (Virasana, Hero or Rock Pose) for easy access to the playing surface of the gong.

If the gong is played while standing, the gong teacher assumes a modified Tadasana or Mountain pose in which the feet are hip width apart with the pelvis in a neutral, balanced position and the navel point pulled slightly in. An inner alignment of the spine is maintained from the base to the crown of the head.

In either seated or standing position, the shoulders are relaxed and the heart remains open. The movement of the arms initiates from the heart, moves through the shoulders and then into the wrists. In yoga, the arms and hands are considered to be the work organs of the heart chakra and take its energy into the outside world.

To maximize the energy transfer from the heart into the playing of the gong, the shoulders and the wrists are opened and made flexible by various yoga asanas such as Gomukhasana (Cow Pose), Garudasana (Eagle Pose), Urdhava Baddha Anguilasana (interlaced hands, arms over the hand with palms inverted).

Asana Sequence for Playing the Gong

Playing the gong effectively requires that there be no energy blocks in the shoulders, elbows and wrists of the gong player that prevent the fluid transfer of prana from the heart into the gong. According to yogic thought and Ayurvedic principles, the blocks in the major joints of the body can be released through a series of exercises known as *pavanmuktasana*, or asanas that free the movement of prana.

While there are several dozen asanas in the pavanmuktasana series, the following sequence of eight exercises systematically address the major areas of the body affected by playing the gong: hands, wrists, elbows, shoulders and chest.

Hands To Fists

Sitting or standing, extend the hands out in front of the body, horizontal to the shoulders. Stretch and tense the fingers of both hands. Then close the fingers over the thumbs to make tight fists. Repeat 10 times.

Wrist Bends

Sitting or standing, repeat the above arm position. Now bend the wrists so the fingers point up, and then bend the wrists so the fingers point down. Repeat 10 times.

Wrist Rotations

Sitting or standing, repeat the above arm position. Make a fist of the right hand around the thumb and rotate 10 times in one direction. Then reverse the direction and rotate again 10 times. Repeat with the left hand. Now repeat with both fists at the same time.

Elbow Forward Bends

Sitting or standing, bring both arms straight out in front with the palms up. Bend both arms at the elbows and touch the fingers to the shoulders. Then straighten the arms again. Repeat 10 times.

Elbow Side Bends

Sitting or standing, bring the arms out from the shoulders, parallel to the ground with palms up. Bend the elbows and touch fingers to the shoulders. Then straighten the arms out again. Repeat 10 times.

Shoulder Rotations

Sitting or standing, bring the fingers to the top of the shoulders. Keep the hands on the shoulders and circle the shoulders forward 10 times. Then circle backwards 10 times. Make the circles so the elbows touch in front of the chest as you rotate the shoulders.

Shoulder Lifts

Sitting with the legs stretched out, make fists of the hands and move the arms from the shoulders, keeping the elbows straight, up to a 60 degree angle and back down to a 60 degree angle. Alternate the arms so the right arm is up and the left arm is down and so on. You can inhale up and exhale as the arms come down. Repeat 20 times.

Heart Pumps

Standing, or ideally squatting on the floor, interlace the fingers and clasp the hands together and raise the arms straight over the head, elbows straight, and then sweep the arms down. Move in a pumping motion, inhaling up and exhaling down. Repeat 20 times.

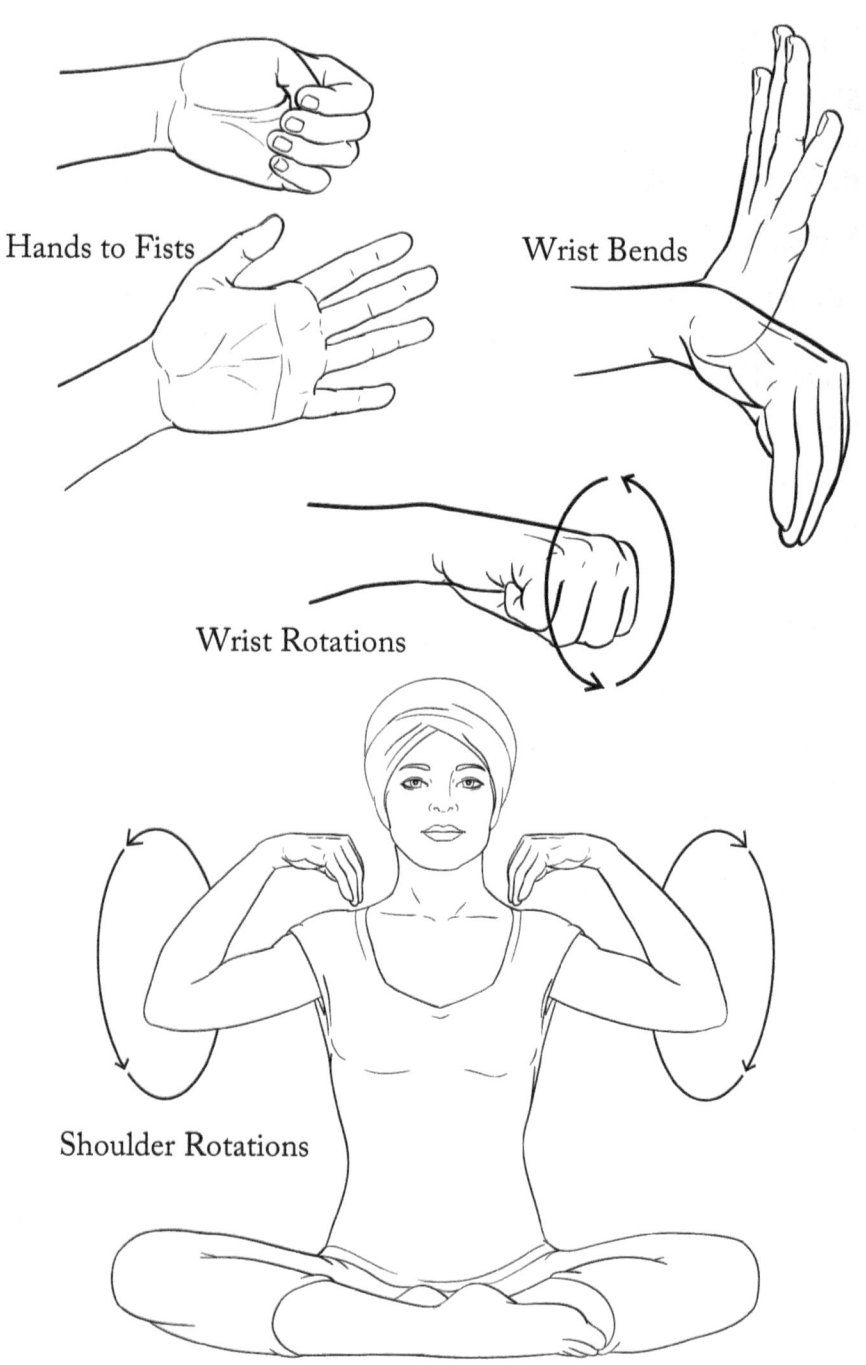

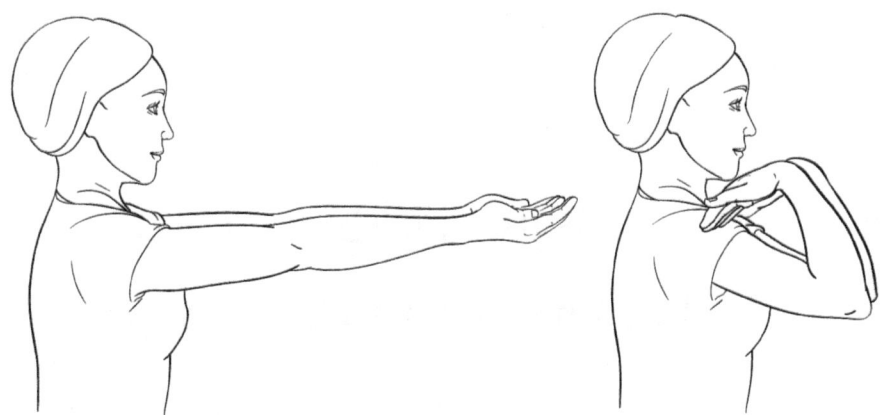

Elbow Forward Bends

Elbow Side Bends

Heart Pumps

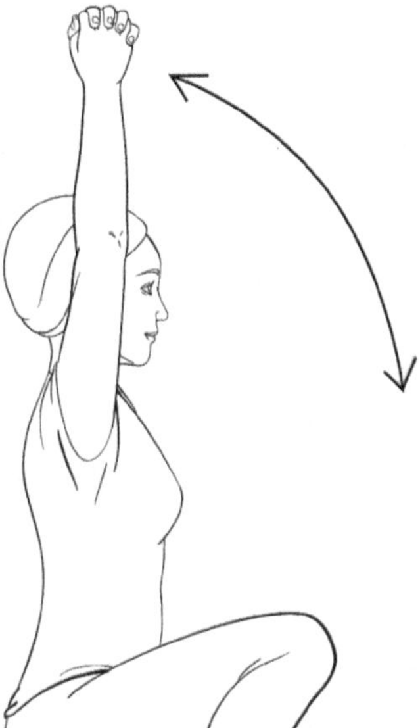

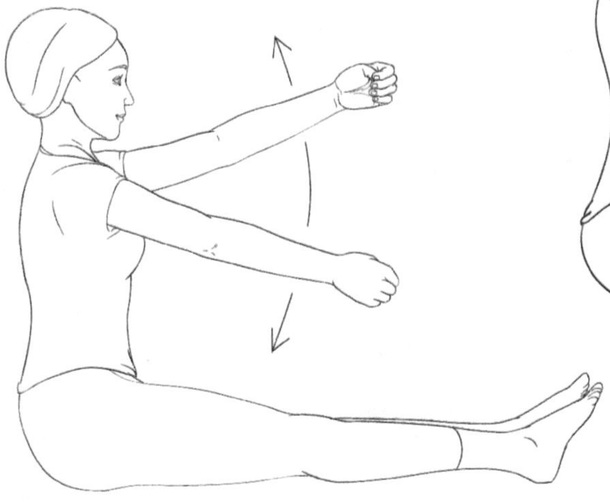

Shoulder Lifts

With every breath,

The sound of love surrounds us.

Rumi

Pranayama and the Gong: Playing for the Energy Body

The relationship between the sound of the gong and the energy body exists because all sound is essentially the expression of prana, the vital energy of the universe. The primal sound in yoga, the sound of OM, is the highest level of sound vibration that created the universe of time, space, and form.

This original cosmic sound came into existence through the force of prana (*prana shakti*), and so it is sound that is the original instrumentality of the expression of all prana, the energy that causes every atom to move and every breath to be taken. It is sound that is the powerful and original vehicle for prana (energy and consciousness), and so it is sound that we work with to master the energy body or pranamaya kosha.

As Swami Satchidananda said, "Physical sound can lead you to the inner vibrations of prana. Prana is the cause of all sound, and sound is the expression of prana." The intrinsic relationship between prana (vital life force) and sound underlies all creation, and is fundamental in playing the gong for all yoga practices and especially the practice of pranayama.

The relationship between sound and prana extends throughout the energy body and affects all aspects of yogic anatomy, including the elements (tattvas), the five basic energies (vayus), the energy channels (nadis), and the energy centers (chakras).

Sound, Prana and the Five Tattvas

The five *tattvas*, or elements, of the material world are earth, water, fire, air and ether (space). Prana is transferred through the five tattvas and is made available to the living organism through one of the five senses associated with that element.

For example, prana is transferred through the element of earth and the sense of smell in the food we eat. Some foods, such as leafy greens, are high in prana while other foods, such as decaying meat, are low in prana.

Prana is transferred through the element of water and the sense of taste by the fluids we drink. Some fluids are high in prana, such as mountain streams, while others are low, such as stagnant water.

Prana comes to us through the element of fire and the sense of sight through light and heat, such as the prana present in sunlight. Environments full of light, such as deserts, are high in prana while areas low in natural light, such as confined spaces, are low in prana.

Prana is transferred through the element of air and the sense of touch through the air we breathe and feel of wind on the skin. Again, environments that are airy invite circulation and are high in prana while places with poor air quality are low in prana.

Finally prana is transferred through the element of space, or ether, and assimilated through the sense of hearing. Sounds that expand and move freely through space in harmony are higher in prana than sounds that are discordant, damped or muffled.

In the same way the five elements or tattvas move from the grossest (earth) to the subtlest (ether), so does prana become more refined as we move from the fundamental sense of smell to the developed sense of hearing, and similarly from the grossest carrier of prana, food, to the subtlest carrier of prana, sound.

Sound carried through the element of ether and perceived by the sense of hearing, as well as the unheard sound (*anahata*) that transcends the physical senses, is the most subtle and ethereal component of the pranamaya kosha. It is through using sound with breath control and awareness (*pranayama*) that we can strengthen, balance, and expand our energy body.

The Energy Body and Yogic Anatomy

The energy body or pranamaya kosha has a structure much the same way that the physical body has its anatomy of organs, glands and bones. The three major components of the energy body anatomy are the vayus (primary energies that move through the pranamaya kosha), the nadis (the subtle energy channels that carry the prana or vital life force), and the chakras (the energy centers that transform prana). The gong may be used in relation to all these components of yogic anatomy to create healing and transformation.

The Five Vayus and the Gong

Within the pranamaya kosha, or the body of the breath, reside five primal energies or **vayus** called the *pancha pranas*. These five vayus, were described hundreds of years ago in the *Chandogya Upanishad* (II.13.6) as the gate keepers to the heavenly world. They represent the five basic types and movements of energy within the body and, when they are mastered, they open the gateway to enlightenment as well as insuring radiant health and well-being.

The five vayus are primarily affected by the breath and emotions and may also be influenced through sound and playing the gong. Whenever the gong is played, one or more of the vayus or primal energies is affected and can be strengthened or balanced depending upon how the gong is played.

The five vayus were originally named and described as follows:

- **Prana Vayu** (that which goes everywhere)
  Responsible for reception or taking in, including breath, food, and sensory input. Prana Vayu is distinguished from universal Prana or *maha prana* in the practice of pranayama.

- **Apana Vayu** (that which takes away)
  Responsible for elimination: what should (or should not) be eliminated, and when to eliminate or release.

- **Samana Vayu** (that which takes what's required to where it is needed)

Responsible for nourishment and assimilation throughout the body

- **Udana Vayu** (that which leads up)
Responsible for speaking, movement, and the elevation of energy.
- **Vyana Vayu** (that which makes things distinct)
Responsible for sensation, as well as lifting, grasping, and throwing.

Prana Vayu

Prana vayu is the incoming energy as represented by the inhalation of the breath. It is initiating, propulsive, and activating in nature. It is localized at the area of the heart, between the larynx and the diaphragm. The element of prana vayu is fire, the ability to move and transform. The prana vayu is associated with perception, everything that comes into the body, be it seeing, eating or otherwise bringing in, and fulfills the subtle function of mental energization. It affects the heart, lungs and brain and gives energy and vitality. When unbalanced or deficient, it creates addictive behavior, misdirected actions and attempts to find wholeness outside of the self.

Prana Vayu and the Gong

Prana vayu is activated by the initiating strike on the gong. It is the energy that brings the sound of the gong into being. It begins as we make the strike toward the gong and is released with initial sound of the gong. It is the birthing of the sound of the gong that activates the prana vayu in the listener. When the prana vayu is present in the sound of the gong, it brings us into time and starts the journey within. The primary playing area of the gong that contains the prana vayu is the upper half of the gong, between the center and below the rim, as well as to the far side of the player.

Apana Vayu

Apana vayu is the downward energy as represented by the exhalation of the breath. It is releasing, relieving, and relaxing in nature. It is localized below the navel and in the lower half of the body. The element of apana vayu is earth, the ability to ground and stabilize. The apana vayu is associated with elimination; everything that must leave the body or mind, be it bodily wastes, reproductive fluids, the birth of a child, as well as old ideas, beliefs, and experiences, and it fulfills the subtle function of mental elimination. It affects the reproduction and elimination systems and gives detachment and dispassion. When unbalanced or deficient, it creates fear, depression and stagnation of the self.

Apana Vayu and the Gong

Apana vayu is activated by the decaying sound of the gong after the strike. It is the energy that takes the sound of the gong away as it fades. Apana vayu begins as we release the contact of the mallet from the gong and allow our own energy to release into the sound of the gong. It is the lessening and declining of the sound of the gong that activates the apana vayu in the listener. When the apana vayu is present in the sound of the gong, it brings us into the relationship of time as it decays and comes to an end. The primary playing area of the gong that contains apana vayu is the lower half, between the center and the rim, as well as to the inside area near the player.

Samana Vayu

Samana vayu is the balancing moving energy as represented by the retention of the breath. It is circular, digestive, and distributive in nature. It is localized at the area of the navel, around the stomach and intestines. The element of samana vayu is water, the ability to transport and assimilate. The samana vayu is associated with digestion and assimilation of everything that comes into the body be it food, knowledge or experiences, and fulfills the subtle function of mental absorption. It affects the digestive organs and gives balance and concentration. When unbalanced or deficient, it creates attachment and greed, and a tendency to hold onto beliefs and emotions that do not serve us.

Samana Vayu and the Gong

Samana vayu is activated by the circular striking of the gong. It is the energy that smoothly assimilates and distributes the integrated sound of the gong. It expresses itself as we strike the gong in a balanced and coordinated manner, moving energy and sound around and around the center of the gong. It is the gentle roaring of the gong that creates a balanced and continuous sound in the listener. When the samana vayu is present in the sound of the gong, it brings a state of fullness and richness where all that is needed is present. The primary playing area of the gong that contains the samana vayu is the area around the center of the gong.

Udana Vayu

Udana vayu is the upward moving energy as represented by the exhalation of the breath after retention. It is positive, transformational, and expressive in nature. It is localized in the upper chest and throat and moving up into the head and beyond. The element of udana vayu is air, the ability to move and flow. The udana vayu is associated with speech upon exhalation and everything that comes up and out of the body, be it spoken words or any forms of self-expression or self-elevation. It fulfills the subtle function of mental expansion and raising the consciousness. It affects the sensory organs in the head area and gives enthusiasm and joy. When unbalanced or deficient, it creates pride and scattered thinking, and an inability to awaken spiritual potentiality.

Udana Vayu and the Gong

Udana vayu is activated by the upward striking of the gong. It is the energy that lifts and raises the sound and rhythm of the gong. It expresses itself as we strike the gong in an elevating and energetic manner, sending energy and sound higher and higher. It is the sparkling sound of the gong that creates a sense of joy and excitement in the listener. When the udana vayu is present in the sound of the gong, it brings a state of high spirits and positive thoughts and an experience of being larger than we are. The primary playing area of the gong that contains the udana vayu is the area near the top of the gong and below the rim.

Vyana Vayu

Vyana vayu is the outward moving energy as represented by the suspension of the breath after inhalation. It is expansive, migratory, and peripheral in nature. It is localized in the limbs of the body and moves the vital energy of the heart (blood) and lungs (breath) to all areas of the body. As such, the vyana vayu is responsible for the experience of all sensation. The element of vyana vayu is ether, the ability to create and enter into space. The vyana vayu is associated with movement and circulation and everything that moves through the body and mind, be it fluids, nerve impulses, feelings or ideas. It fulfills the subtle function of mental circulation and creates a healthy exchange and balance throughout the individual. It affects muscular and nervous movement and gives agility and flexibility. When unbalanced or deficient, it creates separation, dissipation, alienation and disintegration, and an inability to unite with others and to create a connection with the world outside.

Vyana Vayu and the Gong

Vyana vayu is activated by the outward striking of the gong. It is the energy that takes the sound of the gong out and away. It expresses itself as we strike the gong from the center to edge, sending energy and sound farther and farther away. It is the expanding sound of the gong that creates a sense of boundless space in the listener. When the vyana vayu is present in the sound of the gong, it brings us into union and dissolves the boundaries between the listener and the sound. The primary playing area of the gong that contains the vyana vayu is right below and all around the rim of the gong.

Balancing the Vayus: Point-to-Point Breathing

A simple yoga practice to balance the vayus with the gong is to breathe consciously from point to point in the body during a guided relaxation as the gong is played. The practice begins by inhaling from the feet up to the crown of the head, and then exhaling from the crown of the head back down to the feet. The inhale-exhale cycle is repeated 2-3 times.

Then the breath is inhaled from the ankles to the crown of the head and exhaled back down to the ankles 2-3 times. The breath sequence continues moving upward from point to point through the body (ankles, knees, base of spine, etc.) until the third eye point is reached, at which time the sequence reverses as the breath is exhaled downward from point to point (throat, heart, navel point, etc.).

The gong is played in such a way to mimic and connect the movement of breath through the different areas of the body, almost as if the human body were superimposed on the gong surface with the head near the top rim and the feet near the bottom rim.

Point-to-Point Breathing Relaxation Practice

Begin by having students relax on their backs and connect to the breath as the diaphragm rises and falls. Guide the students to inhale from a specific point in their body up to the crown of their head and then exhale down from the crown back to that point. The inhale and exhale are measured by the strike of the gong as the breath is moved up and down the body.

Repeat each breathing point once or twice and then move to the next point in the body as described in the routine. The gong is struck in different areas as specified to balance the different areas of the body, the chakras and the vayus.

- Inhale, visualizing the breath entering the **bottom of the feet** as the gong is struck in an *upward* direction *above rim at the bottom of the gong*. Continue inhaling with the sound as the breath is drawn up to the crown of the head.

Point To Point Breathing

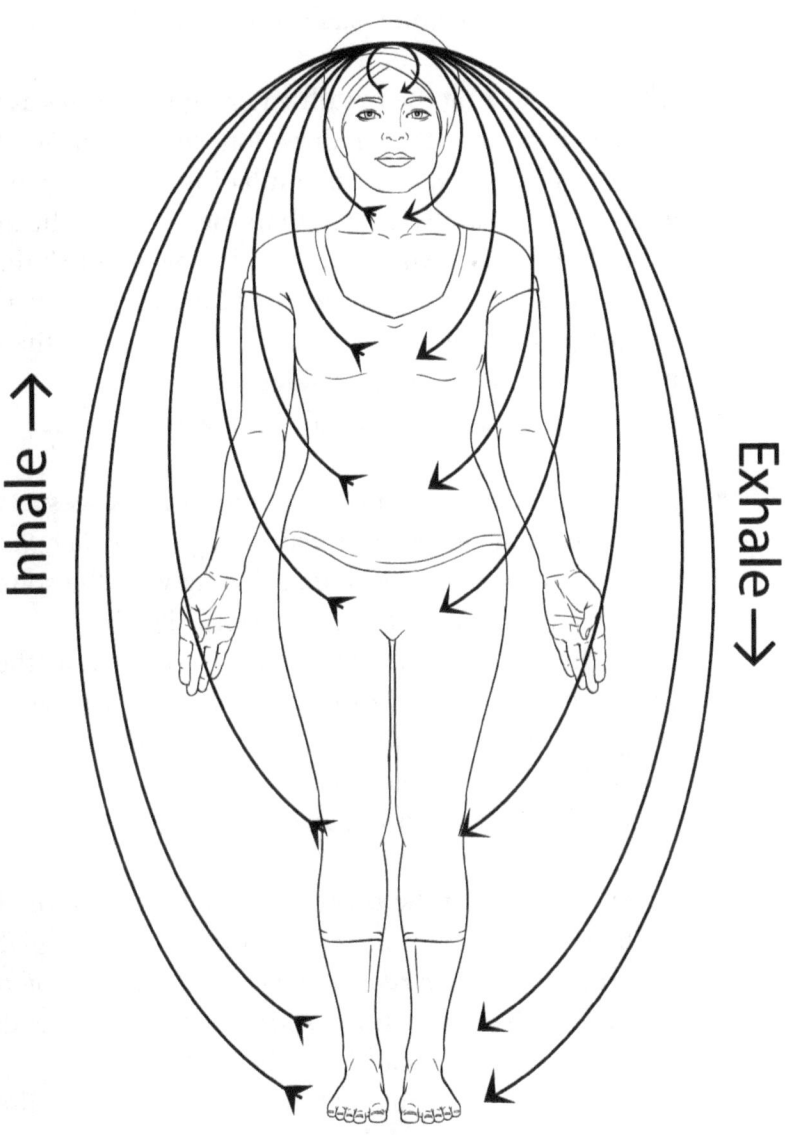

- From the crown, exhale the breath slowly out as the gong is struck in a *downward* direction *below the rim at the top of the gong*. Continue exhaling with the sound as the breath is pressed back down to the **bottom of the feet**.
- Repeat the breath and visualization with the gong.

- Inhale, visualizing the breath entering the **ankles** as the gong is struck in an *upward* direction *slightly higher than the bottom of the gong*. Continue inhaling with the sound of the gong as the breath is drawn up to the crown of the head.
- From the crown, exhale the breath slowly out as the gong is struck in a *downward* direction *below the rim at the top of the gong*. Continue exhaling with the sound as the breath is pressed back down to the **ankles**.
- Repeat the breath and visualization with the gong.

- Inhale, visualizing the breath entering the **knees** as the gong is struck in an *upward* direction *slightly higher than at the bottom of the gong*. Continue inhaling with the sound as the breath is drawn up to the crown of the head.
- From the crown, exhale the breath slowly out as the gong is struck in a *downward* direction *below the rim at the top of the gong*. Continue exhaling with the sound as the breath is pressed back down to the **knees**.
- Repeat the breath and visualization with the gong.

- Inhale, visualizing the breath entering the **base of the spine** as the gong is struck in an *upward* direction *slightly higher than the previous strike and below the center of the gong*. Continue inhaling with the sound as the breath is drawn up to the crown of the head from the knees.
- From the crown, exhale the breath slowly out as the gong is struck in a *downward* direction *below the rim at the top of*

the gong. Continue exhaling with the sound as the breath is pressed back down to the **base of the spine**.
- Repeat the breath and visualization with the gong.

- Inhale, visualizing the breath entering the **navel point** as the gong is struck in an *upward* direction *slightly below the center of the gong*. Continue inhaling with the sound as the breath is drawn up to the crown of the head.
- From the crown, exhale the breath slowly out as the gong is struck in a *downward* direction *below the rim at the top of the gong*. Continue exhaling with the sound as the breath is pressed back down to the **navel point**.
- Repeat the breath and visualization with the gong.

- Inhale, visualizing the breath entering the **heart** as the gong is struck in an *upward* direction *slightly above the center of the gong*. Continue inhaling with the sound as the breath is drawn up to the crown of the head.
- From the crown, exhale the breath slowly out as the gong is struck in a *downward* direction *below the rim at the top of the gong*. Continue exhaling with the sound as the breath is pressed back down to the **heart**.
- Repeat the breath and visualization with the gong.

- Inhale, visualizing the breath entering the **throat** as the gong is struck in an *upward* direction *higher than the previous strike and above the center of the gong*. Continue inhaling with the sound as the breath is drawn up to the crown of the head.
- From the crown, exhale the breath slowly out as the gong is struck in a *downward* direction *below the rim at the top of the gong*. Continue exhaling with the sound as the breath is pressed back down to the **throat**.
- Repeat the breath and visualization with the gong.

- Inhale, visualizing the breath entering the **third eye** as the gong is struck in an *upward* direction *between the previous strike and the rim of the gong*. Continue inhaling with the sound as the breath is drawn up to the crown of the head.
- From the crown, exhale the breath slowly out as the gong is struck in a *downward* direction *at the top of the gong below the rim*. Continue exhaling with the sound as the breath is pressed back down to the **third eye**.
- Repeat the breath and visualization with the gong.

Now reverse the journey by directing the exhale to move systematically back down through the different body points: third eye, throat, heart, navel point, base of spine, knees, ankles, and bottoms of feet. To end, let the breath relax and enjoy the balance created in the body.

The Three Major Nadis and the Gong

Within the energy body or pranamaya kosha, is a network of energy channels called **nadis**. In yogic anatomy, the nadis are rivers of energy that flow through the energetic or subtle body, much like the concept of meridians that carry *chi* in Eastern medicine. These energy channels carry prana or vital life force and play a key role in the awakening of the Kundalini energy of spiritual awareness. When the gong is played, these nadis can be cleared and the listener experiences an increased energy flow into previously blocked areas.

This increased flow of prana through the nadis and the resulting increase in vital energy is one way the gong serves as a healing instrument. In addition, the movement of prana through the nadis awakens, balances, and strengthens the chakra system. The functioning of the nadis is enhanced by breathing practices (pranayama), cleansing disciplines (shatkarmas), and the sound of the gong.

Occasionally the sound of the gong produces tingling sensations or movement of energy in the body. These sensations often occur as the sound of the gong clears blockages in the nadis that may have existed since birth or resulted from traumas.

Most yogic texts say there are 72,000 nadis that carry prana through the subtle or energy body. Of the 72,000 energy channels, there are 14 major nadis used in the practice of Ayurveda and yoga therapy. Of these, three major nadis, the Ida, the Pingala, and the Sushmna, play an important role in the pranamaya practices associated with the playing of the gong and the energy body:.

Ida: The Lunar Energy Channel

The Ida Nadi is associated with the right hemisphere of the brain and the left side of the body or the feminine or lunar polarity. In pranayama practices, breathing through the left nostril is said to increase the flow of prana through the Ida Nadi that creates a receptive, intuitive, and subjective state of consciousness that favors mental activities. The Ida Nadi brings coolness to the mind and body and makes the parasympathetic nervous system dominant.

Pingala: The Solar Energy Channel

The Pingala Nadi is associated with the left hemisphere of the brain and the right side of the body and the masculine or solar polarity. In pranayama practices, breathing through the right nostril is said to increase the flow of prana through the Pingala Nadi that creates a projective, analytical, and objective state of consciousness that favors physical activities. The Ida Nadi brings warmth to the mind and body and makes the sympathetic nervous system dominant.

Sushmna: The Central Energy Channel

The Sushmna Nadi is associated with the integrated whole brain and the transcendence of polarities. In pranayama practices, breathing equally through both nostrils is said to increase the flow of prana through the Sushmna Nadi to create a neutral, balanced, and centered state of consciousness that favors spiritual activities. The Sushmna Nadi brings equanimity and awareness and is associated with the central nervous system.

Swara Yoga, The Flow of Prana and the Gong

The human body follows a natural rhythm in which the flow of prana alternates between the Ida Nadi and the Pingala Nada every hour to 2½ hours, depending upon the individual's biorhythms. When the left nostril is open and the breath flows primarily through the left side, the Ida Nadi is active. When the right nostril is open and the breath flows primarily through the right nostril, the Pingala Nadi is dominant.

While the breath pattern changes from right to left and left to right naturally, we can use pranayama techniques as well as applying pressure points to control which nostril the breath is primarily flowing through and thus control which side of the brain is most active during a Gong Yoga class or meditation.

One simple way to control the flow of breath while the gong is being played during relaxation is to lie on one side of the body to open the opposite nostril (lying on the left side opens right nostril;

lying on the right side opens left nostril).

Another way to activate the Ida or Pingala Nadi during a gong relaxation is to make the sound of the gong dominant in the right ear to activate the Pingala Nadi or in the left ear to activate the Ida Nadi. This can be done by closing close off sound in the right ear and open the flow of prana through the Ida Nadi, or lying on the left side to close off sound in the left ear and open the flow of prana through the Pingala Nadi. More subtly, the gong can be played so that its sound is strongest in the right ear to activate the Pingala Nadi or strongest in the left ear to activate the Ida Nadi.

To Open the Flow of the Ida Nadi with the Gong

Block the right nostril and inhale through the left nostril. Then block the left nostril and exhale through the right nostril. Strike the gong at percussion point 10 with the inhalation and at percussion point 4 with the exhalation. This can be done for 3-7 minutes to open the flow of prana through the Ida Nadi.

To Open the Flow of the Pingala Nadi with the Gong

Block the left nostril and inhale through the right nostril. Then block the right nostril and exhale through the left nostril. Strike the gong at percussion point 2 with the inhalation and at percussion point 8 with the exhalation. This can be done for 3-7 minutes to open the flow of prana through the Pingala Nadi

To Open the Flow of the Sushumna Nadi with the Gong

Practice the previous exercise for the Ida Nadi for 3 minutes. Then practice the previous exercise for the Pingala Nadi for 3 minutes. Play the gong as specified for both exercises. Then begin breathing through both nostrils. On the inhale play up the vertical axis of the gong with short multiple strikes, starting at percussion point 6 and ending at percussion point 12 at the top of the inhale. On the exhale, make one strong strike to percussion point 0 (down). Repeat this breathing and gong pattern for 3 minutes.

The Seven Chakras and the Gong

Within the energy body or pranamaya kosha, are a series of transformational energy centers known as the chakras. Most yoga traditions postulate seven major chakras that align along the Sushumna, or the major central energy channel. The chakras serve as transformers for the prana moving through the Ida and the Pingala nadis, changing and altering the energy to create different frequencies and vortices of power that affect all the levels (koshas) of existence, including the physical body (organs, nerve plexuses, endocrine glands, etc.), the emotional body (psychological states, mental attitudes), the knowledge body (levels of consciousness), and the bliss body (samskaras and tendencies from previous lives).

The chakras hold the keys to achieving the ultimate goal of yoga, integration, union and transcendence, and all the practices of yoga are involved in the balancing and aligning the energies of the chakras, including the use of mantra and sound.

There are many mantras and sounds that resonate with the different energy centers, and this resonance holds a particular frequency for each chakra.

Because of this intimate relationship between sound frequencies and chakras, the gong is a powerful instrument for opening and balancing the flow of energy through them. As the gong is played with its wide range of complex frequency patterns, the chakras come into a natural resonance. It is as if there were a million notes being played simultaneously until the perfect melody is struck for each specific chakra.

The chakras make up one of the richest conceptual frameworks in yoga, and through working with the chakras with various yoga practices and the sound of the gong, we can affect and transform the three bodies - Physical, Subtle, and Causal - as well as all the attendant domains of these bodies, including the organs, glands, physical conditions, psychological states, sensory experiences, and karmic lessons.

Chakras and the Physical Body

Chakra	Physical Body (1) Location (2) Nervous Plexus (3) Endocrine Gland (4) Body Associations (5) Physical Ailments
First **Muladhara**	1. Perineum, base of spine 2. Coccygeal Plexus 3. Adrenals 4. Bones, feet, leg, immune system, colon, rectum 5. Constipation, hemorrhoids, obesity, sciatica
Second **Svadhisthana**	1. Sacral spine 2. Sacral Plexus 3. Gonads 4. Bladder, genitals, kidney, prostrate, uterus 5. Pelvic or low back pain. Urinary, sexual problems
Third **Manipura**	1. Navel 2. Solar Plexus 3. Pancreas 4. Digestive system, liver, muscles 5. Diabetes, hepatitis, indigestion, ulcers
Fourth **Anahata**	1. Center of chest 2. Heart Plexus 3. Thymus 4. Arms, hands, heart, lungs 5. Asthma, circulatory system, heart
Fifth **Vishuddha**	1. Throat 2. Pharyngeal Plexus 3. Thyroid, parathyroid 4. Neck, shoulders 5. Ear, nose and throat problems
Sixth **Ajna**	1. Center of head, brow point, root of nose 2. Hypothalamus, Autonomic Nervous System 3. Pituitary (Pineal) 4. Eyes 5. Eye problems, headaches, sinusitis
Seventh **Sahasrara**	1. Center of head, anterior fontanel 2. Cerebral Cortex, Central Nervous System 3. Pineal (Pituitary) 4. Brain, Nervous System 5. Symptoms without physical cause

Chakras and the Subtle Body

Chakra	Subtle Body
	(1) Kosha (2) Vayu (3) Tattva (element) (4) Tanmatra (sensory expression)
First Muladhara	1. Anamaya Kosha 2. Apana Vayu 3. Prithvi Tattva (Earth) 4. Smell
Second Svadhisthana	1. Pranamaya Kosha 2. Apana Vayu / Vyana Vayu 3. Apas Tattva (Water) 4. Taste
Third Manipura	1. Pranamaya Kosha 2. Samana Vayu 3. Agni Tattva (Fire) 4. Sight
Fourth Anahata	1. Manomaya Kosha 2. Prana Vayu / Vyana Vayu 3. Vayu Tattva (Air) 4. Touch
Fifth Vishuddha	1. Vijnanamaya Kosha 2. Udana Vayu 3. Akasha Tattva (Ether) 4. Hearing
Sixth Ajna	1. Vijnanamaya Kosha 2. Five Vayus (Prana, Apana, Udana, Vyana, Udana) 3. Manas (Mind) / Light 4. Thought
Seventh Sahasrara	1. Anandamaya Kosha 2. Transcendent 3. Transcendent 4. Transcendent

Chakras and the Causal Body

Chakra	Causal Body (1) Goals (2) Karmic Lessons (3) Needs
First Muladhara	1. Survival, security, stability, grounding, prosperity, physical health, family 2. Living in the material world 3. To be present, to feel
Second Svadhisthana	1. Sexuality, creativity, fluidity, pleasure, bonding, relaxation, worthiness, emotional connection 2. Creatively manifesting through relationship 3. To let go, to be sexual, to create, to live
Third Manipura	1. Manifestation, strength of will, purpose, power, accomplishment, vitality, taking action, energy 2. Empowerment through self-acceptance 3. To act, to move, to commit
Fourth Anahata	1. Neutrality, balance, compassion, integration, appropriate boundaries 2. Trusting in the benevolence of the universe 3. To give, to receive, to forgive, to love
Fifth Vishuddha	1. Self-expression, truth, communication, resonance, harmony 2. Speaking and living the Truth 3. To express, to listen, to empathize
Sixth Ajna	1. Intuition, perception, visualization, imagination, focus, insight, understanding 2. Seeing the One beyond dualities 3. To know the truth, to see the unseen, to live in an expanded state of reality
Seventh Sahasrara	1. Consciousness, enlightenment, surrender, union, merger, transcendence 2. Connecting to the infinite 3. To be at One, to align with the divine

Playing the Gong for the Chakras

When playing the gong to affect the chakras, there are five considerations for the Gong Yoga teacher:

- The nature of the gong
- The playing areas of the gong
- The rhythm of the gong playing
- The intention of the player
- The state of the listener

Nature of the Gong and the Chakras

The chakras have been associated in various sound healing practices with specific frequencies and musical notes. It should be noted, however, that in the original practices of yoga and the descriptions of the chakras, these sound frequencies were never specified. Indeed, when the chakras were first discussed in the Upanishads, the Western musical scale was not even known. As a result, much of what has been speculated about chakras having specific tone frequencies cannot be verified through the teachings of yoga.

Nevertheless, there are gongs that are approximately or exactly tuned to the commonly postulated frequencies for the chakras. The temptation is to speculate that when a specific gong is played that is tuned to the frequency of a chakra, it would then resonate or balance that particular chakra's energy.

While there is little doubt that the size, composition and tuning of a gong will have specific effects on the chakra system, it is an oversimplification to say that "Gong A" will balance the fourth chakra or "Gong C" will balance the sixth chakra. In reality, any gong is capable of balancing any chakra if played properly.

For those who wish to compare and experiment with the tuned gongs on the various chakras, the following table shows the Paiste Planetary gongs that are most closely tuned to the frequencies that are usually associated in the various sound healing modalities with the seven chakras:

Chakra	Frequency	Paiste Planetary Gong
First (Root)	194.18 Hz	Sidereal Day (194.71 Hz)
Second (Sacral)	210.42 Hz	Synodic Moon (210.42 Hz)
Third (Solar Plexus)	126.22 Hz	Sun (126.27 Hz)
Fourth (Heart)	136.10 Hz	Earth (136.10 Hz)
Fifth (Throat)	141.27 Hz	Mercury (141.27 Hz)
Sixth (Third Eye)	221.23 Hz	Venus (221.23 Hz)
Seventh (Crown)	172.06 Hz	Platonic Year (172.06 Hz)

Another way to use the planetary gongs with the chakras, is to follow the traditional association of the seven visible planets with the seven chakras according to Jyotish, or Indian Astrology. This approach would be more in alignment with Vedic thought and yoga practices than the association of the chakras with the sound frequencies. By following this method in the following table, it is interesting to note that only the fifth chakra remains consistent with both these approaches:

Chakra	Paiste Planetary Gong
First (Root)	Saturn
Second (Sacral)	Jupiter
Third (Solar Plexus)	Mars
Fourth (Heart)	Venus
Fifth (Throat)	Mercury
Sixth (Third Eye)	Moon
Seventh (Crown)	Sun

Playing Areas of the Gong and the Chakras

The area of the gong that is struck also affects the different chakras. According to Yogi Bhajan, master of Kundalini Yoga and the gong, the seven major chakras may be accessed through the gong playing area by superimposing a map of the chakra system as it aligns up within the body, moving from bottom to top.

In this manner, the first chakra would be located at the bottom of the gong, directly above the rim area. The second chakra would be right above the first chakra and the third chakra right below the bottom center of the gong. The fourth chakra would be around the center of the gong and the fifth chakra above the top of the center of the gong. The sixth chakra is closer to the top of the gong and the seventh or crown chakra is right beneath the top rim of the gong. The aura that surrounds the energy body and the seven chakras is associated with the rim area around the gong face.

This mapping of the chakras over the face of the gong corresponds to the ancient astrological mapping of the areas of the body to the signs of the zodiac, or the Cosmic Man, with the first sign (Aries) corresponding to the head and so on down to the last sign (Pisces) associated with the feet.

This also follows one of the major teachings of esoteric philosophy that states the physical body perfectly aligns with the subtle or energy body. This one to one mapping of the physical body with the energy body is illustrated by the widely recognized medical condition known as *phantom limb* in which a person seems to feel an arm or leg long after it has been amputated.

These playing areas of the gong allow the Gong Yoga teacher to access individual chakras as well as working with the energetic pairing of the chakras. The following chakras are often associated as working together through their higher and lower frequencies, and both these chakras may be balanced by alternating strikes between their respective areas: Chakras 1 and 7; Chakras 2 and 6; Chakras 3 and 5; Chakras 4 and 8 (aura area around the rim).

Chakras and the Playing Areas of the Gong

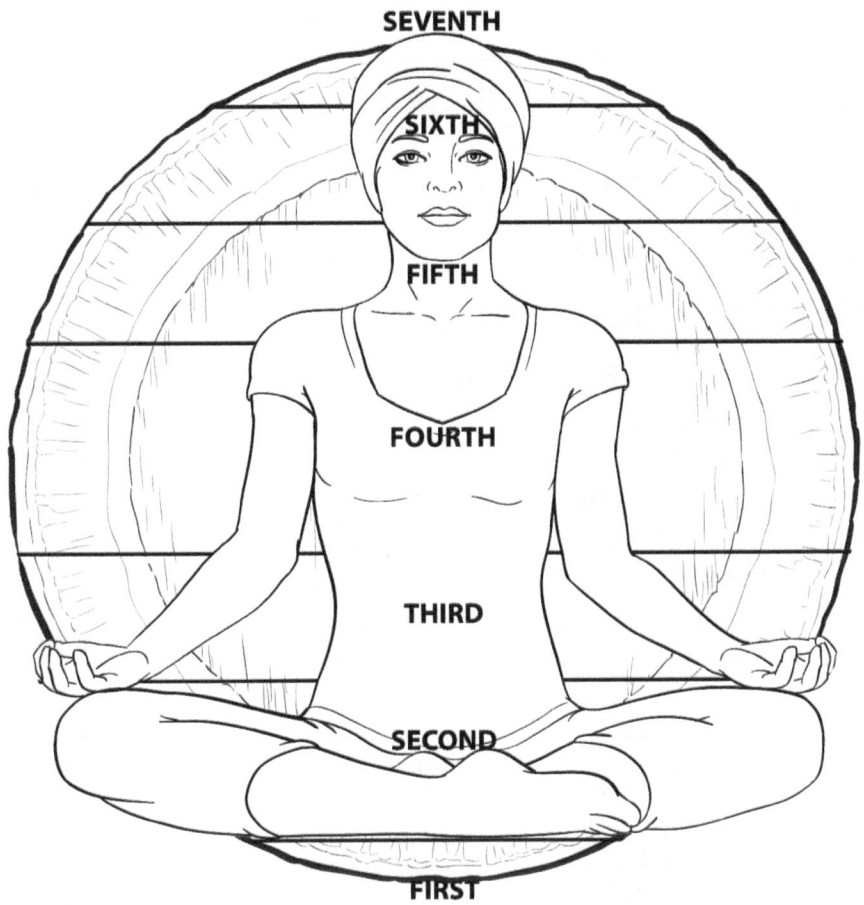

Playing Rhythms and the Chakras

One of the more consistent and observable effects of the gong on the chakras follows this basic rule: The faster the rhythm, the higher the chakra affected. A slow rhythm resonates with the lower chakras while a fast rhythm moves energy to the higher chakras.

The relationship between a slow rhythm and a fast rhythm is dependent upon the player's individual baseline rhythm, but it does follow a ratio of 3:5:7. In other words, a slow rhythm has a value of "3" and a medium rhythm would be "5" (or about 1.67 times as fast as a slow rhythm). A fast rhythm would be "7" (or proportionately about 2.33 times as fast as a slow rhythm or 1.4 times faster than the medium rhythm).

Again, these proportions are relative to the individual rhythm of the player and not an absolute measurement. Most simply, the more the rhythm is increased, the higher the chakra that is affected.

Playing Intention and the Chakras

Like all sound produced, the intention behind the production of the sound is paramount. An angry and unfeeling gong player will have little success in working with the heart chakra regardless of the frequency of the gong, the area of the gong that is struck, or the rhythm of the playing.

An effective way to play the gong for a specific chakra is to play in a manner that is in accordance with the major keyword of each chakra, such as the following table shows.

Chakra	Intention Keyword
First (Root)	Security
Second (Sacral)	Connection
Third (Solar Plexus)	Manifestation
Fourth (Heart)	Compassion
Fifth (Throat)	Expression
Sixth (Third Eye)	Perception
Seventh (Crown)	Unity

For example when playing the gong for the fifth chakra, the intention of the player is to express and create with a desire to communicate. When playing for the second chakra, the intention is to connect the listener to the sound and create a relationship between the player and the gong, and so on.

Condition of the Listener and the Chakras

The condition of the listener is perhaps the paramount factor in how the gong affects the chakras. This condition to a large degree is based upon the karmas of the listener, the life experiences, and whether there is a deficiency or sufficiency of prana in the various energy centers.

The listener's condition prior to hearing the gong, however, can be shaped by the practice of yoga practices specific to the various chakras and the use of mantras, affirmations, and visualizations. In other words, the Gong Yoga teacher can create a fertile ground and set expectations for the listener's experience of the gong as it relates to the chakras that are affected.

For example when playing for the heart chakra, a focus on backbends or devotional chanting might precede the playing of the gong.

The Energy Body and the Breath Cycle

The practice of yoga actually begins with the cycle of breath that repeats over 20,000 times a day. It is breath, or more properly the prana through the breath, that creates movement (asana), energy (pranayama), sound (mantra) and thought (meditation). Working with the basic cycle of inhalation and exhalation while using the gong is the first step to using sound to enhance the energy body (pranamaya kosha) as well as our yoga practice.

The gong may be used to guide and enhance the basic movements of pranayama that make up the breathing cycle of inhalation (**puraka**), exhalation (**rechaka**) and retention or suspension (**kumbhaka**). In the practice of yoga, this full pranayama cycle consists of four phases:

- Puraka (inhalation)
- Abhyantara kumbhaka (retention of breath after the inhale)
- Rechaka (exhalation)
- Bahya kumbhaka (suspension of the breath after the exhale)

A simple way to use the gong in a pranayama practice is to signal each breath phase. At the beginning of the inhale (*puraka*), the gong is gently struck and the inhale continues until the sound disappears. The breath is then retained in (*abhyantara kumbhaka*) for a time equal to the inhale. Then the gong is struck and the exhale begins (*rechaka*) and continues until the sound disappears. The breath is then suspended out (*bahya kumbhaka*) for a time equal to the exhale. The cycle begins again when the gong is struck again.

In addition to serving as a timer, the gong can also be played during one or both of the kumbhaka phases while the breath is held in or held out.

By consciously suspending the breath, the whole system becomes controlled as we stop nervous impulses in different parts of the body and start to harness the brain wave patterns. Since it is the movement of prana (breath) that enables the mind to think, when this movement is suspended, the mind becomes quiet. During deep meditation the breath naturally becomes suspended for a short period of time, and it is in this interval that pranayama truly occurs. As Patanjali, the author of the Yoga Sutras, observed: "Pranayama is the **cessation** of the movement of inhalation and exhalation." (*Yoga Sutras* 2:49).

It is during this period of breath cessation that the gong can be used to re-pattern consciousness and clear *samskaras*, or past life energies. When the breath is suspended out, for example, it is common for deep fears associated with death to come to the surface. The gong can overlay those fears with its own pranic and sonic field and effectively neutralize them when played correctly. When the breath is retained in, the gong can be played to encourage the circulation of prana from the heart outward into the energetic body. This could be done, for example, by playing from the center of the gong outward while the breath is held in, and then released or exhaled with a definite strike.

Ultimately, the gong can be played during pranayama to induce the state of *kevala kumbhaka* (or *stambhavritti pranayama*), in which the breath is simply stopped, without breathing in or breathing out. According to the yogic texts, this state is the highest form of pranayama practice.

"He who is successful in the absolute state of kevala kumbhaka, without breathing in or out, finds nothing in the three worlds beyond his reach." (*Vasishtha Samhita*)

"When the breath can be stopped for three *ghatikas* (75 minutes), the yogi can realize all the attainments he wishes for without doubt." (*Shiva Samhita* 3, 62)

While such a state may seem unreachable to the ordinary practitioner, the sound of the gong can create a transcendent trance-like experience in which the movement of the breath seems to disappear or is paused almost indefinitely. When the gong is played in a repetitive, slow, and even manner for an extended period of time, allowing the hypnotic sound to build softly like a far-reaching wave, the practitioner can sit in meditation and focus on the movement of the breath at the tip of the nose and enter a state approximating non-breathing or kevala kumbhaka.

Pranayama Practices and the Gong

All the formal yoga pranayama practices may be enhanced through the sound of the gong. In effect, the gong multiplies and directs the flow of prana through the energy body when played with the various breathing exercises.

While there are hundreds of pranayama techniques and variations, they can all be categorized as to the effects they create, much like the asanas or physical postures, as either being cooling (Langhana), warming (Brimhana), or balancing (Samana). Pranayamas can also be categorized as to a secondary effect of being tranquilizing, vitalizing or balancing. Depending upon the combinations of these various qualities for each pranayama, the gong may be played at certain rhythms, volumes and playing areas to enhance the effects of each pranayama.

The following table of the twelve most common pranayama practices in the Hatha and Kundalini traditions indicates the qualities of each one and the gong practices that accompany it.

Pranayama	Quality	Effect	Sound	Rhythm
Sitali or Sitkari	Langhana	Tranquilizing	Soft to Medium	Slow
Chandra Anga	Langhana	Tranquilizing	Soft	Slow
Chandra Bhedana	Langhana	Tranquilizing	Soft	Slow
Bhramari	Langhana	Tranquilizing	Soft	Medium
Kapalabhati	Langhana	Vitalizing	Medium	Fast
Nadi Shodhana	Samana	Balancing	Soft to Medium	Slow
Agni Pran Breath of Fire	Samana	Vitalizing	Medium to Loud	Fast
Viloma	Samana	Varies	Varies	Varies
Ujjayi	Brimhana	Balancing	Soft to Medium	Slow to Medium
Surya Bhedana	Brimhana	Vitalizing	Medium	Medium
Surya Anga	Brimhana	Vitalizing	Medium	Medium
Bhastrika	Brimhana	Vitalizing	Loud	Fast

Sitali or Sitkari Pranayama (Cooling or Hissing Breath)

Sitali pranayama, or the cooling breath, and Sitkari pranayama, or the hissing breath, reduce body heat and soothe the emotions. They are differentiated from most pranayamas in that the inhalation occurs through the mouth. These two breath practices quiet the mind and create muscular relaxation that can help induce sleep. The practices also remove pain in the head and face areas, reduce blood pressure and acidity, and detoxify the liver. In the *Hatha Yoga Pradipika* (2:58), it is said that practicing Sitali pranayama cures an enlarged stomach or spleen, lowers excess fever, counteracts poisons and reduces hunger and thirst. Sitkari pranayama has the added benefit of keeping the teeth and gums healthy.

Breath Technique: Sitali Pranayama is performed by extending the tongue outside the mouth and curling it so it forms a tube (if unable to curl the tongue, focus on the center of the extended tongue) and then drawing the breath in over the tongue. The tongue is then drawn in, the mouth closed, and the exhale is through the nose.

For Sitkari pranayama, the teeth are lightly held together and the lips separate so the breath is drawn through the teeth. The exhale is done through the nose with the mouth closed.

Gong Technique: The gong is played softly at a medium-low volume with a slow rhythm. The intention behind the playing is cooling and calming.

Chandra Anga (Moon Path Breath)

Chandra Anga, more popularly known as the Moon or lunar breath, works primarily with the Ida Nadi to bring about coolness, relaxation and tranquility. The breath works powerfully on the right hemisphere of the brain, and has been useful in accessing mental patterns and unconscious habits. This predominantly activates the parasympathetic nervous system and *manas shakti*, the mental or lunar energy.

Breath Technique: The breath is controlled by inhaling and exhaling through the left nostril while blocking the right nostril. The breath may be continuous. An advanced practice is to retain the breath as long as the inhale and the exhale (1:1:1 ratio). The ratio can slowly be increased with practice to 1:2:2 and eventually 1:4:2.

Gong Technique: The gong is played to activate the Ida Nadi during the pranayama practice by striking the gong at the beginning of each inhale and exhale. When inhaling through the left nostril, the gong is played with an upward strike at percussion point 9. When exhaling through the left nostril, the gong is played with a downward strike at percussion point 9. The rhythm should be slow to allow for a full inhale and exhale and the volume is soft. The intention behind the playing is receptivity and nurturing.

Chandra Bhedana (Moon Piercing Breath)

Chandra Bhedana, more popularly known as the Moon Piercing breath, works with Ida Nadi to bring about relaxation and alertness. The breath works on the right hemisphere of the brain and the parasympathetic nervous system.

Breath Technique: The breath is controlled by inhaling through the left nostril and exhaling through the right nostril, alternately blocking off the nostril not being used. The breath may be continuous for excellent effect. An advanced practice is to retain the breath for as long as the inhale and the exhale (1:1:1 ratio). The ratio can slowly be increased with practice to 1:2:2 and eventually 1:4:2.

Gong Technique: The gong is played to activate the Ida Nadi during the pranayama practice by striking the gong at the beginning of each inhale and exhale. When inhaling through the left nostril, the gong is played with an upward strike at percussion point 9. When exhaling through the right nostril, the gong is played with a downward strike at percussion point 3. The rhythm should be slow to allow for a full inhale and exhale and the volume is soft. The intention behind the playing is relaxation and releasing.

Bhramari (Humming Bee Breath)

Bhramari pranayama, more popularly known as the humming bee breath, produces a soothing effect on the mind and nervous system while also reducing blood pressure and ameliorating throat ailments. It has traditionally been used to deal with anxiety, anger and insomnia, as well as healing body tissues following operations. Significantly in the practice of Gong Yoga, the breath facilitates the awareness of all sound and subtle vibrations and awakens psychic sensitivity. In the *Hatha Yoga Pradipika* (2:68), it is said that by practicing this pranayama one becomes "lord of the yogis and one's mind is absorbed in bliss."

Breath Technique: The breath is done by with the lips gently closed, teeth slightly relaxed and not touching, and the jaw muscle loose. The ears are closed with the index or middle finger pressing the earflaps closed, with the elbows out to the sides and the upper arms parallel to the grounds. Inhale through the nose and with the mouth closed, exhale slowly with a deep steady hum in the head, smooth, even and continuous. The sound is soft and deep, making the front of the head vibrate.

Gong Technique: The gong is played with a medium soft and sweeping swishing sound by lightly and rapidly moving the mallet around the surface. The intention behind the playing is inclusive and encompassing so that the two sounds blend outside and inside.

Kapalabhati (Forehead Shining Breath)

Kapalabhati, also known as the Skull Shining or Forehead Shining Breath, is one of the six basic cleansing practices of yoga (the shatkarmas). The name refers to its invigoration of the entire brain, and particular the frontal lobe (forehead). The breath is cleansing and energizing while simultaneously slowing down the activity of the mind (*vrittis*).

Breath Technique: The breath is distinguished by an active exhale and passive inhale. The inhale occurs naturally after the exhale is forced. The inhale and exhale together take about one second, and are done consecutively for 20 repetitions, or one round. The breath is then inhaled fully and retained comfortably and then exhaled normally. After a few regular breaths, up to 5 to 10 more rounds may be performed. Advanced practices include retaining the breath at the end of a round and applying *mulabandha* (root lock), as well as increasing the number of repetitions in a round and the number of rounds.

Gong Technique: The gong is played in rhythm with the fast breath, almost like a quick tapping on the gong and medium loud in volume, with each strike signaling an exhale. The gong may be played at any percussion point, but typically gets best results when played with upward strikes below percussion point 12. At the end of the round (10-50 repetitions), the gong is struck once loudly to signal the end and the breath is retained comfortably as the sound decays. The intention behind the playing is to create an upward flow of invigorating and clearing energy.

Nadi Shodhana (Alternate Nostril Breath)

Nadi Shodhana, more popularly known as alternate nostril breathing, is one of the most beneficial and basic pranayamas practiced in yoga. The name translates as purification of the energy channels (*nadis*) and prepares the subtle body to handle the increased flow of prana that comes from the practices of yoga. Moving the breath through the left nostril opens the Ida Nadi while right nostril breathing is associated with the Pingala Nadi. When both major nadis are balanced and open, meditation begins and intuition awakens. The practice brings a balance to the sympathetic and parasympathetic nervous systems and balances the emotions. When this pranayama is practiced with the gong, there is an experience of prana moving more directly and openly into the energy channels with the breath.

Breath Technique: The breath is controlled by first inhaling through the left nostril while blocking the right nostril, then exhaling through the right nostril while blocking the left nostril. Then the breath is inhaled through the right nostril, with the left nostril still blocked. Complete the cycle by exhaling through the left nostril with the right nostril blocked. The cycle repeats by inhaling through the left nostril and continuing as desired.

Gong Technique: The gong is played to activate the Ida and Pingala Nadis during the pranayama practice by striking the gong at the beginning of each inhale and exhale. When inhaling through the left nostril, the gong is played with an upward strike at percussion point 9. When exhaling through the right nostril, the gong is played with a downward strike at percussion point 3. When inhaling through the right nostril, the gong is played with an upward strike at percussion point 3. When exhaling through the left nostril, the gong is played with a downward strike at percussion point 9. The rhythm should be slow to allow for a full inhale and exhale and the volume is soft to moderate. At the end of the practice, still or silence the gong, inhale through both nostrils, retain the breath, and then exhale as the gong is struck near the center. The intention behind the playing is balance and purity.

Agni Pran (Breath of Fire)

Agni Pran (fire breath), more popularly known as Breath of Fire, accompanies many Kundalini Yoga exercises and is independently used as a separate pranayama practice. The breath is vitalizing and balancing, encouraging both detoxification and alertness, and focuses the mind while oxygenating the body. The benefits of this breath are numerous and as it activates the energy center at the solar plexus (the third chakra) which is associated with the fire element in yogic physiology. It burns the impurities in the body and purifies the nervous system. The breath is enjoyably energizing.

Breath of Fire helps detoxify the lungs, mucous linings, blood vessels, and other cells. It expands the lung capacity and increases physical endurance. It balances sympathetic and parasympathetic nervous systems and strengthens the nerves. It expands and energizes the body's electromagnetic field. It focuses the mind, elevates the mood, and alleviates depression. It reduces addictive impulses for foods, drugs, and smoking. It boosts the immune system and stimulates glandular secretions. It creates a harmonic resonance among all the body's systems and synchronizes its biorhythms. It purifies and oxygenates the bloodstream within three minutes of practice.

Breath of Fire may be done as a separate practice to energize the physical and energetic bodies.

Breath Technique: The breath is distinguished by a quick and equal active inhale and active exhale through the nose as if lightly panting with the mouth closed. There is an equal intensity and length of the inhale and the exhale, at the rate of 1 to 3 breaths per second. The heart is lifted and the solar plexus lightly dances with the breath, yet the movement is not forceful or contractive. The breath is rhythmical (equal length between inhale and exhale) and quick (1 to 3 breaths per second) so a continuous light panting breath through the nose is accomplished without strain. While breath of fire may consist of 60 to 180 inhalations and exhalations per minute, it is physiologically one continuous breath. The lungs are never completely emptied or filled during the breath. Instead, air is baffled or vibrated in and out of the lungs by the motion of the diaphragm at the navel point.

Gong Technique: The gong is played playing moderately fast and at a medium to loud volume. The rapid rhythm of the breath can be matched with a similar quick playing rhythm on the gong, striking the surface at the rate of 1 to 2 times per second. The strikes are generally made upward near the top of the gong. The intention behind the playing is to energize, balance and uplift.

The following pranayama practice demonstrates the effectiveness of using the gong to amplify the effects of the Breath of Fire.

Agni Gong (Fire Gong) Exercise

Assume a meditative posture and raise the arms over the head and separate the hands (palms facing out) about two feet (30 centimeters) apart. Close the hands into fists with the thumbs outside and pointing at a 45-degree angle upward. Close the eyes and focus at the brow point or third eye (sixth chakra).

1. Begin the breath of fire, lifting the arms up and very slightly back to open the heart. Continue the breath of fire at the same rhythm throughout the exercise.
2. After 30 seconds, begin playing the gong steadily and moderately fast at the top of the gong, about two thirds up from the center and below the rim at a light to moderate volume.
3. After another 30 seconds, increase the rhythm and slowly increase the volume.
4. After another 30 seconds, again increase the rhythm rate and volume.
5. After another 30 seconds, hold the rhythm rate but increase the volume so that the sound of the breath disappears into the sound of the gong.
6. After 30 seconds at the loud volume, make 2 or 3 powerful strikes with a crashing and releasing sound at points of your choosing. Then remove the mallet from the gong and let the sound decline naturally while continuing the Breath of Fire.
7. After 30 seconds as the sound diminishes, inhale very deeply and retain the breath and posture for 15 seconds or until the sound disappears into silence.
8. Exhale. Relax the hands down into a meditative posture. Meditate at the third eye for 60 seconds or more.

Viloma Pranayama (Segmented Breath)

Viloma Pranayama, also known as segmented breath, is done by pausing the breath during inhalation and/or exhalation. The pausing segments the breath and creates a finer control of the breathing process and deepen the relationship to the experience of prana. It is an excellent practice to extend breath duration and retention and to expand breath capacity. The pauses may occur in different ratios to create specific effects. The most commonly practiced Viloma breath ratios and their benefits are summarized in the following table.

Viloma Breath Ratios	Effects
1 Part In : 4 Parts Out	Meditative, balancing, purifying
4 Parts In : 1 Part Out	Energizing, elevating, clearing
4 Parts In : 4 Parts Out	Simulating, strengthening
3 Parts In : 3 Parts Out	Neutralizing, heart opening
4 Parts In : 8 Parts Out	Releasing, eliminating, calming
8 Parts In : 1 Part Out	Energy, stress relieving
8 Parts In : 4 Parts Out	Builds energy and focus
8 Parts In : 8 Parts Out	Creates endurance and stamina
10 Parts In : 10 Parts Out	Balances brain and metabolism
16 Parts In : 16 Parts Out	Complete glandular tune-up

Breath Technique: The breath is a complete inhale and exhale, but paused, or interrupted, by stopping the inhale or exhale for one second. The breath is not sniffed or forcefully pulled in or pushed out. Instead the breath is simply stopped several times, according to the ratio practiced. For example, on a 4:4 ratio, the inhale is paused when the breath is ¼ inhaled, then paused at ½ inhaled, then again ¾ inhaled and finally paused when fully inhaled. The exhale is done by letting ¼ of the breath exhale, then ½ the breath exhaled, then ¾ the breath exhaled, and finally all the breath is exhaled.

Gong Technique: The gong is struck for each part of the inhale and the exhale, approximately every 2-3 seconds, giving time for a one-second pause between each part. At the end of the inhale and the exhale cycle, the sound of the gong fades for 3-5 seconds before the next cycle. On the inhale cycle, the gong is sequentially struck above the center of the gong and graduating to near the top, stepping up the volume almost imperceptibly with each strike. On the exhale cycle, the gong is sequentially struck below the center of the gong and descending to near the bottom, diminishing the volume with each strike. The intention behind the playing is to create a rhythmical and almost hypnotic state by pulsing the gong.

Ujjayi (Psychic Breath)

Ujjayi Pranayama, also known as the psychic breath and translated as the victorious breath, opens the subtle states of the mind and may be practiced in any position (standing, sitting, lying down) and with many techniques (asana, mantra, and meditation). The breath reduces hypertension, mental tension, turns the mind inward and increases psychic sensitivity. In the *Hatha Yoga Pradipika* (2:51-53), it is said that practicing Ujiya pranayama removes phlegm, stimulates digestive fire (*agni*), and removes disorders of the energy channels (*nadis*) and tissues (*dhatu*).

Breath Technique: The breath is controlled by gently contracting the glottis in the back of the throat so that a soft hiss or whisper is created in the throat (audible only to the practitioner). This is best accompanied by a simultaneous light contraction or natural lift in the abdomen with a minimum of effort. Both inhale and exhale are long and deep through both nostrils.

Gong Technique: The gong is played to imitate the hissing sound of the breath by building the sound through small rapid strikes in one area, varying the rhythm from slow to moderate and increasing and decreasing the sound back and forth between soft and medium loudness. The intention behind the playing is watery and soothing.

Surya Bhedana (Sun Piercing Breath)

Surya Bhedana, more popularly known as the Sun Piercing breath, works with Pingala Nadi to increase warmth and strengthen projection. The breath works on the left hemisphere of the brain and the sympathetic nervous system. In the *Hatha Yoga Pradipika* (2:50), it is said that practicing this pranayama purifies the brain and destroys the imbalances present in the vata (wind) dosha.

Breath Technique: The breath is controlled by inhaling through the right nostril and exhaling through the left nostril, alternately blocking off the nostril not being used. The breath may be continuous for excellent effect. An advanced practice is to retain the breath for as long as the inhale and the exhale (1:1:1 ratio). The ratio can slowly be increased with practice to 1:2:2 and eventually 1:4:2.

Gong Technique: The gong is played to activate the Pingala Nadi during the pranayama practice by striking the gong at the beginning of each inhale and exhale. When inhaling through the right nostril, the gong is played with an upward strike at percussion point 3. When exhaling through the left nostril, the gong is played with a downward strike at percussion point 9. The rhythm should be slow to medium and allow for a full inhale and exhale and the volume is medium. The intention behind the playing is outgoing and focusing.

Surya Anga (Sun Path Breath)

Surya Anga, also known as the Sun or solar breath, works primarily with Pingala Nadi to bring about focus, awareness and energy. The breath works powerfully on the left hemisphere of the brain, and has been useful in expressing mental creativity and connecting with the external world. This predominantly activates the sympathetic nervous system and *prana shakti*, the vital or solar energy. In the *Hatha Yoga Pradipika* (2:63), it is said that "when the body is tired, inhale through the right nostril."

Breath Technique: The breath is controlled by inhaling and exhaling through the right nostril only while blocking the left nostril. The breath may be continuous for excellent effect. An advanced practice is to retain the breath as long as the inhale and the exhale (1:1:1 ratio). The ratio can slowly be increased with practice to 1:2:2 and eventually 1:4:2.

Gong Technique: The gong is played to activate the Pingala Nadi during the pranayama practice by striking the gong at the beginning of each inhale and exhale. When inhaling through the right nostril, the gong is played with an upward strike at percussion point 3. When exhaling through the right nostril, the gong is played with a downward strike at percussion point 3. The rhythm should be slow to medium and allow for a full inhale and exhale and the volume is medium. The intention behind the playing is warming and elevating.

Bhastrika (Bellows Breath)

Bhastrika, also known as Bellows Breath because of the forceful pumping, is the most energizing pranayama of yoga. The breath is heating and builds the internal fire of the physical and pranic body. It increases oxygen levels, reduces carbon dioxide, stimulates the metabolic rate, and flushes out wastes and toxins while massaging the organs, particularly the liver, and improves digestion and elimination.. In the *Hatha Yoga Pradipika* (2:66-67), it is said that practicing this pranayama arouses kundalini and breaks open the three psychic pranic knots (*granthis*) so the kundalini may rise.

Breath Technique: The breath is a strong active exhale and inhale with an exaggerated movement of the diaphragm and abdomen. One inhale and exhale cycle takes two seconds for beginners and may be increased to one cycle per second and then two cycles per second. Generally the breath is practiced in rounds of 10 to 30 breaths and from 5 to 10 rounds. Beginners may start by breathing through both nostrils. Eventually the breath is done for one round through the left nostril only, ending with a deep inhalation through the left nostril and retention. Then a round is done for the right nostril only. Finally a round is done with both nostrils. The cycle of left, right, and both nostrils may be repeated from 3 to 10 times. At the end of a round, the inhaled breath may be retained for several seconds and then exhaled suspended out for several seconds. Normal breathing may be practiced between the rounds.

Gong Technique: The gong is played in rhythm with the breath, loudly and quickly, with a strike for each breath cycle (inhale and exhale). The strike rate will be one to four times every two seconds, and should be played louder than the sound of the powerful breath. The gong may be played at any percussion point, but typically gets best results when played with upward strikes above the center of the gong (Up 0 percussion point). If retention of the breath is practiced, at the end of the round the gong is struck loudly one time to signal the end of the round and the breath is inhaled and retained comfortably as the sound decays. The gong is struck again to signal the exhalation. If suspension of the breath follows after exhalation, the gong is struck at the end of the suspension when it is time to inhale again. The intention behind the playing is fiery and forceful.

The Gong Yoga Teacher's Practice: Pranayama

The Gong Yoga teacher creates a relationship with prana, the breath, and the gong by practicing pranayama while playing. Simply stated, the player breathes into the gong and with the gong.

Consciously breathing while playing the gong is a powerful pranayama practice for the player. By connecting the breath to the movement of the mallet and the playing process, the Gong Yoga teacher can direct prana into the sound, as well as cultivate and conserve their own prana. The more prana the player can bring into the playing process through conscious breathing techniques, the more transformational the sound becomes.

The conscious breathing can be long deep breathing or it can be a modified Breath of Fire (or Agni Pran) or continuous Ujiya breath as the gong is played rhythmically. For specific single strikes, a conscious inhale occurs when the mallet is pulled away from the surface and the exhalation occurs when the mallet strikes the gong. Breathing the mallet into the gong in this manner creates a pranic charge that is amplified through the sound and reaches the listener.

When the Gong Yoga teacher maintains a conscious awareness of the breath while playing, the prana transferred from the player through the playing of the gong is increased.

Similarly, the students can be instructed to use their breath awareness to bring more prana by consciously directing their breath into different areas of the body as the gong is played. This can be done to create an opening in asana, a release during relaxation, or a focus during meditation that connects sound to breath in a new and powerful way.

I am the taste of the water,

The light of the sun and moon.

I am the sound in the ether,

And the possibility within you.

Bhagavad Gita (7:8)

Mantra and the Gong: Playing for the Emotional Body

Mantra and the sound of the gong affect the manamaya kosha, the layer of existence between the breath body (pranamaya kosha) and the knowledge body (vijnanamaya kosha), thereby creating the bridge from the gross to the subtle practices of yoga. When mantra is used or when the gong is played, the manamaya kosha is strengthened and healed, much like asana for the physical body and pranayama for the energy body.

Because it affects the emotional layer, the sound of the gong can bring emotional releases, especially when heard the first several times. Crying or laughing may be common, as well as experiencing transient states of anxiety, fear, love or bliss, as emotional reorganization is brought about by the sound of the gong.

Gradually as the manamaya kosha interacts with this sound, the various emotional states subside and the general feeling is well-being. From this calm and neutral emotional center, it becomes easier to experience the meditative mind contained in the vijnanamaya kosha.

The relationship between the gong, mantra, the emotional body, and the inner sounds of yoga is one of the most profound in the practice of Gong Yoga.

The Gong, Mantras and the Science of Naad

All sound has a common origin with the universal sound current. All music, all spoken words, all mantra possess to some degree a fundamental frequency and a specific sound essence that is known as **Naad**. This sound essence is the vibrational harmony that connects the finite to the infinite. When we hear sounds that are closely aligned with this universal resonance known as the Naad, we tune in to the infinite consciousness that is the source of all sound.

Mantras are especially potent vehicles to carry the Naad and were the first recorded yoga technique, predating the more common practices (at least in the Western world) of asanas and pranayama. As powerful as mantras are for creating a change in consciousness due to their ability to align us with the Naad, it is the Gong that most closely approximates the Naad in its purest state and vibration.

Within the gong are all mantras, all sounds, all words, and all voices, and it is not uncommon for people to experience "hearing" different musical instruments in the sound of the gong. When the gong is used with mantra, we purify and accelerate the effects of the mantra on the manamaya kosha. Using the gong with mantras is one of the most natural expressions of Gong Yoga, and can be achieved in three ways:

- Mantras are played while the gong is played.
- Mantras are chanted while the gong is played.
- Mantras are repeated silently while the gong is played.

Playing Mantras with the Gong

A simple way to experience the power of mantras with the gong is to play recorded mantras and the gong simultaneously. The recorded mantra provides a soundtrack that the gong player can interact with by playing over, under, or along with the recorded sound.

When the gong is played with a recorded mantra, the gong player may interact with the mantra in several ways. One option is to begin playing the mantra before the gong is struck and allow the listener to fully hear the mantra and experience its rhythm and vibration. After awhile, the gong player can begin playing the gong softly in a supporting rhythm or cadence that is consonant with the mantra. At this stage, the sound of the mantra dominates over the sound of the gong that simply serves to accentuate and not obliterate the recorded mantra.

A second option is to start by playing the gong first and then bringing in the sound of the recorded mantra. The gong player plays the gong softly enough so the mantra can be heard, but, unlike the first option, the gong remains the dominant sound and the mantra is experienced almost subliminally.

A third option is to start either with the recorded mantra or the gong, and then alternate the gong playing so that at times the mantra dominates the listener's experience, and at other times the gong is louder than the mantra. Indeed, the gong may eventually completely overwhelm the sound of the mantra until it simply disappears and then magically re-appears as the gong is played softly. The alternating duet between the volume of the gong and the volume of the mantra re-directs the focus of the listener until the two sounds blend into a greater synergistic whole.

When selecting a mantra to play with the gong, consider its rhythm, cadence and strength. A simple mantra is best, as well as a mantra with a strong carrying tone and rhythm that can complement and compete with the powerful sound of the gong.

Chanting Mantras with the Gong

Chanting a mantra as the gong is played increases the prana of the mantra and brings its vibration deeper into the listener's awareness. The active participation between the chanter and the gong player is somewhat akin to the practice of kirtan whereby the voice of the individual is assimilated into the common group sound (supplied by the gong) and produces a sense of sonic communion.

Unlike playing the gong with a recorded mantra, playing the gong with a mantra chanted by one or more individuals requires the gong be played at a volume so the sound of the mantra can be clearly heard. In other words, the gong becomes a partner in the sound current produce by the mantra and neither dominates nor disappears as the mantra is chanted.

Mantras of simple repetitive sounds work best when chanting with the gong, such as bija mantras (seed mantras of one or two syllables) and ashtang mantras (mantras with 8 distinctive sounds).

Amplifying Mantras with the Gong

If the gong is large enough (generally 38 inches or 100 cm), there is the opportunity to chant mantras near the gong when it is not being played and have the sound of the mantra reverberate through the gong and be heard. In this way, the gong serves as a transmitter, amplifier, and transformer of the human voice, translating the spoken mantras into the language of the gong and allowing it to chant with the practitioner.

The ability of the gong to capture any sound in the room and then re-sound it makes it a powerful instrument to have in a yoga class whether it is played or not. Whenever mantras are chanted or music is played in a room with the gong, these sounds are subtly captured and returned by the gong, even when inaudible to the human ear, producing a vibrational complexity that affects the consciousness.

Furthermore, once struck, the vibrations of a gong resonate at the molecular level for *40 years*! For all practical purposes, the gong is always chanting or resonating, regardless if it is being actively played or not.

Silent Mantra with the Gong

Chanting a mantra silently as the gong is played strengthens the subtle body of the practitioner and directs the flow of prana produced by the gong. Similarly to using mantra with asanas and pranayamas, repeating a silent mantra with the gong directs the mind and clears the subconscious.

Mantras consisting of simple repetitive sounds work best when chanting silently with the gong, such as bija mantras (seed mantras of one or two syllables) and ashtang mantras (mantras with 8 distinctive sounds).

The silent use of mantras with the gong works well for people who may have fears or resistance around the sound of the gong, as well as those who may be suffering from traumatic stress or shock. The silent mantra creates a connective link between the listener and the gong that gives a sense of control to the practitioner.

The advantage for the gong player is that silent mantra allows for more freedom in how the gong is played. For the listener, silent mantra can create a deeper internal focus than when mantras are chanted out loud.

Chakra Bija Mantras with the Gong

An effective use of mantras with the gong is to chant the traditional bija (seed) mantra for each chakra while the gong is struck to activate the corresponding chakra. The mantras may be done silently or out loud. They may also be pronounced in such a way to either calm (Langhana) or activate (Brimhana) their energy. The following chart shows the two ways of chanting the mantras and the corresponding areas of the gong to be struck for the seven chakras.

Chakra	Mantra (calming)	Mantra (activating)	Gong Area
First Muladhara	LAM	LANG (lung)	Above bottom rim
Second Svadhishthana	VAM	VANG (vung)	Higher above bottom rim
Third Manipura	RAM	RANG (rung)	Below center
Fourth Anahata	YAM	YANG (yung)	Above center
Fifth Vishuddha	HAM	HANG (hung)	Higher above center
Sixth Ajna	AUM	ONG (ong)	Below top rim
Seventh Sahasrara	Silence	Silence	Silence gong

When chanting the mantras to calm or balance, the ending sound "M" is extended. When chanting to activate these energies, the following pronunciation guidelines are be helpful:

The bija mantra LANG is pronounced *lung* with the 'L' sound produced by placing the tongue behind the upper teeth. The mantra is made up of two sounds that are almost equal in length, 'LA' and 'NG.'

The duration for the two sounds is the same for all the chakra bija mantras. Notice the common sound 'NG' is created by vibrating the sound inside the cranium.

The bija mantra VANG is pronounced *vung* with the 'V' sound produced by the lips as though making a 'FF' sound.

The bija mantra RANG is pronounced *rung* with the 'R' sound produced by curling the tip of the tongue to the roof of the mouth.

The bija mantra YANG is pronounced *yung* with the 'Y' sound produced with the tongue pressed against the soft palate at the front of the roof of the mouth.

The bija mantra HANG is pronounced *hung* with the 'H' sound produced at the back of the throat.

The bija mantra ONG is produced from the back of the throat and the front of the open mouth.

Nada Yoga and the Inner Sounds

Nada Yoga divides sound into the inner sounds, discovered by the yogi in meditation, and the outer sounds, such as music and the gong that are conveyed through the sensory organs. Being able to experience the inner sounds is considered to be the highest form of Nada Yoga.

Yet the use of external sounds, such as practiced in Gong Yoga, can also create a focused awareness and a heightened sensitivity to all vibration that can lead the practitioner to an experience that is similar to that produced by hearing the subtle inner sounds.

These inner sounds have been compared in various yogic texts to external sounds created by musical instruments. By replicating these internal sounds through musical instruments and the gong, we can create an experience of Nada Yoga. The following descriptions from the major works on yoga describe the different stages of the inner sounds.

Hatha Yoga Pradipika

In the first stage, the sounds are surging, thundering and jingling like kettle-drums. In the second stage, the sounds are like the conch and bells. In the final stage, the sounds are like the flute and the bee.

Shiva-Samhita

The first sound is the hum of the bee, then a flute, then a harp and gradually the sounds of ringing bells and then a roar like thunder.

Nadabindu Upanishad

At first the sound is like the gentle ocean, then the kettle-drum and waterfall. Later the sound is like a small drum, then a big bell and a military drum. Finally the sound is that of a tinkling bell, the flute, the harp and a humming bee.

Darsana Upanishad

First the sound of a conch blast (sankha-dhvani), then a clap of thunder, and finally the roaring of a mountain stream.

Hamsa Upanishad

The sounds begin as a whisper, then as a bell. Next the conch, the lute, and the cymbal. Then comes the flute, the drum, and finally roaring thunder.

Although these descriptions differ, the gong can approximate many of these sounds when skillfully played and appears in all of these descriptions at some stage.

Here is a suggested soundscape, from five different yogic texts, to externally re-create the inner sounds heard by the yogi in meditation by using musical instruments, including the gong.

Hatha Yoga Pradipika	Siva Samhita	Nada Bindu Upanishad	Darsana Upanishad	Hamsa Upanishad
Gong	Humming	Gong	Conch	Humming
Drums	Flute	Small Drum	Drums	Bell
Conch	Harp	Big Bell	Gong	Conch
Bells	Bells	Big Drum		Lute
Flute	Gong	Small Bell		Cymbal
Humming		Flute		Flute
		Harp		Drums
		Humming		Gong

The gong can also be played by itself for 2 to 3 minutes through each of the six successive stages, from the subtle to the most profound, moving from top to bottom, as follows:

Stages of Sound	Gong Playing Technique
First	Slow single centering strikes, medium soft
Second	Light sparkling strikes around the top rim
Third	Medium diagonal strikes (percussion points 2 > 8, 10 > 4)
Fourth	Strong center strikes (percussion points Up 0, Down 0)
Fifth	Crashing strikes upper half of gong
Sixth	Light whispering strikes above bottom rim

Shanmukhi (Yoni) Mudra and the Inner Sounds

Shanmukhi mudra may be used to create a state of sensory withdrawal, or pratyahara, to go inward and listen to the inner sounds. The Sanskrit word *shan* means six and *mukhi* means face or gate. Shanmikhi mudra involves using the fingers to close the six gates of perception or openings in the face – the two eyes, two ears, and two nostrils – to limit sensory input. The mudra is also called Yoni mudra as the word *yoni* also means a cave or the womb where sensory impressions are decreased.

How to Do it: Bring the palms in front of the face with the elbows. Close the ears with the thumbs. Close the eyes with the index and middle fingers by gently pressing the eyelids. Inhale deeply and close the nostrils with the ring fingers. Retain the breath as long as comfortable while closing the ears, eyes and nostrils with the fingers. After some time, release the pressure of the middle fingers and slowly breathe out. You can also keep the fingers on the nostrils without closing them to perform this without breath retention. Listen to the silence or inner sounds. Practice 3 to 11 minutes or as long as comfortable, then remove the fingers and lower the arms.

Shanmukhi (Yoni) Mudra and Hearing the Gong

Shanmukhi mudra may also be used to listen to the gong and constitutes a form of gong yoga meditation. The teacher begins playing the gong as students connect to the breath. After a few moments, the students perform Shanmikhi mudra, using the option to not block the nostrils and instead breathing normally. By sealing off the ears and eyes, a new experience of the sound of the gong is created that is deeply internalized in the listener.

Using Other Sounds with the Gong

For the yogi, the gong is not simply a musical instrument to be played or orchestrated with other instruments. Yet its powerful sound can be used with other musical sounds to re-create the the inner sounds of Nada Yoga.

The most obvious examples of gongs as part of a greater sound experience are the traditional gamelan orchestras of Indonesia in which there may be flutes, metal bowls, thick metal bars and other percussion instruments. In keeping with this classical approach, suitable instruments to be used with the gong are other metal percussion instruments, woodwinds, and drums.

In particular, metal bowls and chimes seamlessly complement the gong soundscape, while native flutes and the conch work well during periods of silence. The *sitar* (or harp) and *vina* (zither) are also old friends with the gong. The Australian didgeridoo, while not used in the original yoga practices, creates a contrast of earthly sonorous sounds with the ethereal sound of the gong. In many cases, these instruments are used before or after the gong is played, or during interim periods when the gong is silent.

The Gong Yoga Teacher's Practice: Mantra

Chanting mantras silently and out loud while *playing the gong* can be profound and transformational for both the player and the listener. Just as practicing pranayama without mantra is not pranayama, playing a gong without mantra is simply – well, only playing the gong!

Chanting mantras while playing the gong connects the prana and consciousness of the gong player to the gong and powerfully directs the prana into the sound of the gong and the consciousness of the listeners. In some ways, this is one of the greatest and most powerful secrets of teaching gong yoga.

While chanting mantras out loud may not always be possible or even advisable in some teaching situations and environments, the teacher can always chant a mantra silently as the gong is played. Play in the rhythm and cadence of your silently chanted mantra, and let mantra inform and guide your playing. In this manner, the gong will magnify the effects of the mantra many times over.

Meditation and the Gong: Playing for the Knowledge Body

One of the most effective uses of the gong in the practice of yoga is its ability to induce a state of spontaneous meditation, regardless of the background or experience of the practitioner. Indeed, people who have never had a formal practice or experience of meditation are able to enter into a physiological and psychological state of meditation through the sound of the gong.

Part of its ability to create a state conducive to meditation is that the sound of the gong has an affinity for activating the crown chakra that connects the listener to a consciousness that exists beyond time and space. One of the gong's earliest uses was to be played at the time of death to allow the subtle body to leave the physical body through the crown chakra, as postulated in some yoga teachings.

Throughout its history the gong has also been played to create a heightened state of psychic sensibility. It was played to awaken intuition so that prophets and mystics could more easily foretell the future. The gong was considered to be a portal to God because its playing increased a profound state of intensified sensory perception through sound that allowed the listener to experience the self in a new way.

To understand how the gong can be played for meditation in a yoga practice, we first need to distinguish what yoga practices facilitate the meditative state to occur.

Yoga Techniques and Meditation

The popular Western practices of yoga are drawn from the Hatha and Kundalini traditions, and meditation will be discussed in this context, as opposed to the practices of Raja Yoga as described in the Yoga Sutras.

Essentially in these traditions, meditation occurs as a result of employing the yogic techniques of asana, pranayama, mudra and mantra or sound in a synergistic manner to prepare the physical, energy, and emotional bodies to experience the knowledge body (vijnanamaya kosha). Lets look at these four foundational techniques in the practice of Gong Yoga meditation.

Asana and Gong Meditation

The experience of the gong as played for relaxation is profoundly different then when played for meditation. This difference primarily occurs due to the asana requirement in yoga that meditation can only occur when the body is in an upright-seated posture and not when in a relaxed supine state. In yoga, meditation is the process by which the movement of energy through the spine and chakras opens the higher centers of consciousness. This movement only effectively occurs when the spine of the practitioner is in a perpendicular relationship to the earth's magnetic field so that energy can move upward.

While the gong may be enjoyed in a transformational way when relaxing on the back, the experience is not properly called meditation unless a seated posture is used (including siting in a chair, as long as the spine is in perpendicular alignment). Another consideration is how posture affects our orientation in time. Supine postures, as occur in sleep or deep relaxation, create an orientation to the past, such as in the dream state. Standing positions, such as occur when walking or moving through space, create an orientation toward the future as we move forward. Seated postures, such as occur during reflection and self-absorption, create an orientation to the stillness of the present, which is another characteristic of meditation.

Pranayama and Gong Meditation

Conscious awareness of the breath is a requirement in the practice of Gong Yoga meditation. All meditation begins with a conscious connection to the breath, as the movement of prana is intimately associated with the movement of the mind. Without some sort of breath awareness, at least initially, the state of meditation is difficult to create and maintain.

When the gong is played, one of its major effects is to create a movement of prana through the body. This rhythmical and resonating movement of prana through the sound of the gong deeply affects the nature of the mind and the arising of thoughts. Often the mind seems to stand still or is suspended by the sound of the gong. This occurs because the movement of prana begins to move in accordance with the sound of the gong and not in its usual erratic or vacillating nature. A new pranic pattern is imprinted when the gong is played, and this can be greatly enhanced through a conscious connection with the breath.

If students are challenged by the gong as it begins its energetic re-programming of the body, mind and emotions, it is helpful to remind them to simply create an aware connection to the breath. This breath awareness allows the prana that is moved by the gong to more easily be integrated into the emerging new pattern of energy. When this is accomplished, the meditative mind naturally occurs. In this respect, breath awareness, or a modified form of breath control or pranayama, aids in creating the experience of meditation when listening to the gong. Without the breath awareness, there may be a resistant to the movement of prana that the gong produces and an inability to enter fully into meditation.

Mantra (Sound) and Gong Meditation

Obviously the yogic technique of using sound (or mantra) is paramount in practicing Gong Yoga meditation. The common error in playing the gong for meditation is to assume that one only needs to experience the sound, much like hearing music, to create the desired effect. There is a fundamental difference, however, between hearing and listening, and this difference is vital in the practice of Gong Yoga meditation.

Hearing is a passive process, and sometimes unconscious, whereas listening is active and completely conscious. Listening to the gong is what allows its sound to produce a state of meditation and for the listener to completely merge with the outer and inner sound that is the goal of using mantra and sound in yoga.

Guru Nanak expressed the virtue of listening over 500 years ago when he recited the following in a heightened state of mystical revelation: "Listening, the technology of yoga, and the secrets of the body are revealed. …Listening, and intuitively grasping the essence of Meditation."

Actively listening to the sound of the gong during meditation can be accomplished in several ways. One method, which can also be done when practicing mantra, is to internalize the outer sound into the body or mind. This can be done by localizing or visualizing the sound of the gong into the spine, feeling the sound move through the body and vibrating along the central channel or Sushumna. Another way to is actively listen to the sound as it enters both ears, distinguishing the subtle difference in sound between right and left. Allowing the sound to vibrate inside the head or various other areas of the body also can create a deeper identification with the sound of the gong. Sensing the tactile sensation that sound can create on the surface of the skin, inside the ears, or even the eyelids creates a deeper identification with the sound. Sometimes even sensing the sound moving along the floor and entering the base of the spine can be a profound experience.

If you are visually oriented, the sound can be given colors or allowed to create images at the brow point or third eye. You can also see the sound as it moves around the room and through the body. By exploring other forms of synesthesia, such as tasting or even smelling the various sounds the gong creates, different cognitive pathways open that allow us to deeply listen to the gong in a meditative manner. Primarily, listening to the gong during meditation is a willful and active engagement of the senses to first identify the sound as coming from the outside but ultimately existing inside the listener.

In reality, the sound of the gong only exists in the mind of the listener due to its unique combination of acoustic undertones that is created in playing, and so no two people hear the gong in the same manner. This entirely personal perception of the gong's sound is due to its undertones. These undertones, which are produced when loud tones are sounded together, are known as combination tones. Acousticians consider combination tones to be a physiological phenomenon, rather than an acoustical one, because the tones are actually synthesized within the inner ear of each listener by the vibration of the cochlea, or extremely delicate hairs. The gong thus produces an inner sound as well as an outer sound. It is this dual sound that takes each listener deeper into their own experience of being so that the sound of the gong becomes individually unique to each person and leads them into the inner realm of deep meditation.

Mudras and Gong Meditation

The last technique of Gong Yoga meditation, the performance of mudras, is the most important to create the state of meditation. A mudra is commonly thought of as a hand position or gesture in which the fingers touch each other in order to seal and direct the flow of prana. More generally, mudras may also involve muscular locks (*bandhas*), eye positions or gazes (*drishtis*), and certain body positions (*asanas*).

When various mudras are used in a yoga practice along with the sound of the gong, the movement of prana in the energy body can be optimally directed to produce a state of a state of meditation. Indeed, all gong meditation is primarily mudra-based and, as mentioned, may involve the fingers, eyes, muscular locks, and body positions to integrate the sound of the gong more deeply into the practice. Mudras work primarily to attune and balance the energies of the first three koshas, physical, energetic and mental, so that the knowledge body, the fourth kosha is strengthened.

While mudras are a necessary component of all yogic meditation practices, they play an even more critical role in Gong Yoga Meditation. Without mudras, there can be no experience of meditation using the sound of the gong because the mudras are essential to direct the prana created by the sound to the different areas of the physical and subtle body that support meditation.

There are over 3500 known mudras in the practice of yoga and all of them can be used with the sound of the gong. The gong supports all mudras, and any mudra can more effectively channel the energy of the gong for healing, pranayama, and meditation. Here are a few hand (*hast*) mudras that are known to specifically facilitate meditation with the gong.

Pran Bandha Mudra

An effective hand mudra to use for Gong Yoga meditation is Pran Bandha, which collects, binds and commands the life force (*pran*) that is produced and directed by the sound of the gong. The mudra is performed by holding the two small fingers of each hand meditation down with the thumb and extending the two large fingers up, side by side. The hands are held at shoulder level, palms facing forward. The hands are pulled slightly back so a pressure is created between the shoulder blades and the spine is fukky engaged and lengthened. There is a sense of opening the central channel of the body, or Sushumna, so that energy can rise upward through the body. The eyes are closed and fixed on the tip of the nose. Be aware of the two extended fingers as you listen to the sound of the gong.

Sahasrara Bandha Mudra

There are many variations of Sahasrara mudra in which the hands are interlocked or clasped over the crown of the head. Sahasrara refers to the crown chakra, or the seventh energy center, which exists about four inches about the top of the head. A basic version is to interlace the fingers and bring the hands 4-6 inches (10-15 centimeters) over the top of head. The arms are pulled slightly back so that the hands are over the center of the skull. There is a constant

light pull on the hands as if they could be pulled apart. The eyes roll up to the top of the head as if to look up into the hands. This mudra greatly facilitates the natural opening of the crown chakra that the sound of the gong produces.

Humkara Mudra

This Tibetan Buddhist mudra that crosses the hands over the heart has many different expressions, depending upon how the hands and fingers are held. The mudra brings equanimity, neutrality and balance to the heart and mind. The simplest version has the left hand crossing over the center of the chest and the right hand crosses over the left hand, locking energy at the heart chakra. Another variation is to cross the wrists, not touching, with the thumb tip touching the index finger tip of both hands. Many mudras can be adapted to this practice by performing the same mudra with each hand and then crossing the two hands with the right in front over the left over the heart center.

Gyan Bandha Mudra

This mudra uses the classic Gyan mudra (sometimes called Chin or Jnana mudra) that touches the thumb tips to the index finger tips of both hands. In Gyan Bandha mudra, the two individual circles formed by Gyan mudra are interlocked with each other by joining them together like a chain link in front of the heart. The interlocked circles do not touch each other but float in space. The eyes are one-tenth open and look down toward the interlocked chain. This mudra has the ability to completely still the mind and lock the thoughts and is especially useful when playing the gong in a rhythmical and hypnotic manner.

Mudras for the Chakras

As the gong can be played to activate and access the seven major chakras and different gongs may also be used to work on specific chakras, specific mudras may be held for each of the chakras. You can refer to the section on chakras for how to play the gong for each chakra mudra.

There are many different mudras for the chakras. The following ones are some of the simplest to perform.

First Chakra (Muladhara Mudra)

Technique: Touch the tip of each index finger touch to the tip of each thumb. Extend the other fingers out, touching the sides together. Rest the hands palms down toward the earth. Perform *mulabandha*, or the root lock, by slightly contracting the anal sphincter, sex organs and navel point.

Second Chakra (Swadhisthana Mudra)

Technique: Open the hands, palms up. Hold the right hand below the navel point and above the lap with the palm turned up. Rest the back of the left hand in the right palm. Connect the two thumbs tips together. (Men should reverse the hand position).

Third Chakra (Manipura Mudra)

Technique: Bring the hands together in front of the navel point with the four fingers joined together, tips touching, Pull the hands slightly apart, keeping the fingertips touching. Cross the left thumb over the right thumb. (Men should cross the right thumb over the left thumb.)

Fourth Chakra (Anahata or Lotus Mudra)

Technique: Bring the hands in front of the heart center and join the heels of the palms together. Pull all the fingers back away from each other and then join the sides of the little fingers and thumbs together, making a shape like an open lotus or flower.

Fifth Chakra (Vishuddha Mudra)

Technique: Interlace the fingers with the palms facing up and relaxed in a comfortable position. Connect the thumb tips together and pull them upward to make a circle between the palms and the thumbs.

Sixth Chakra (Ajna Mudra)

Technique: Bring the hands together and join the four fingers by pressing the second knuckle of each finger together. Turn the palms down and pull the thumbs down and touch the thumb tips together. Now extend the middle fingers up straight from the other fingers and touch their two tips together, pointing upward.

Seventh Chakra (Sahasrara Mudra)

Technique: With palms facing down, interlace the fingers and cross the thumbs, left thumb over right thumb. (Men reverse the position.) Extend the little fingers up and touch the tips together.

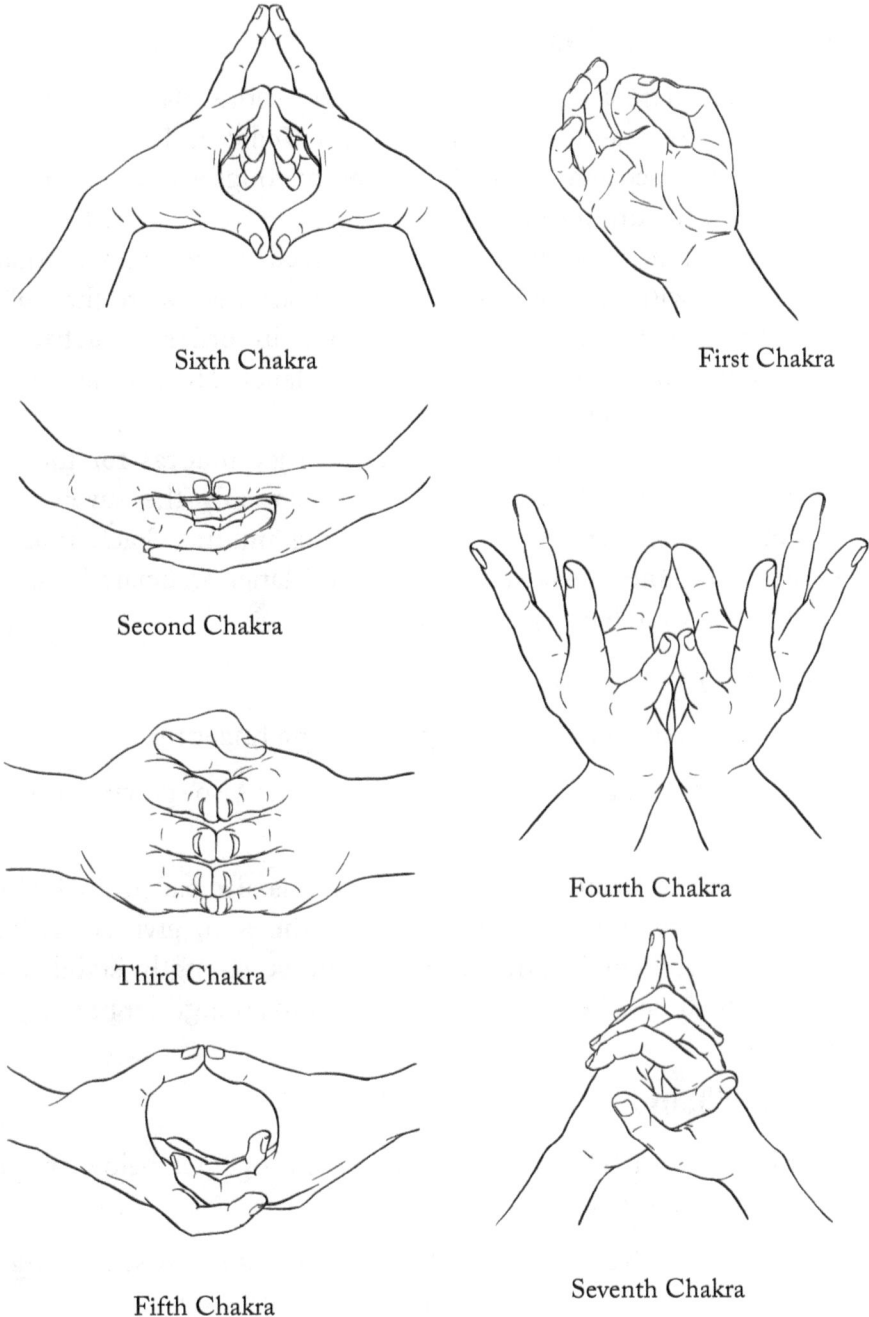

Mudras for the Planets

Given that there are gongs tuned to the various planetary energies, there are also traditional mudras from Vedic or Indian astrology that may be used when specific planetary gongs are played in order to enhance the unique energy of each one.

In addition, any gong can be played in a manner that is consonant with the primary quality associated with that planet according to Vedic (Indian) Astrology in order to activate or balance the energy associated with that planet. The primary playing style for each planet is also specified.

Notice that there are no traditional yogic mudras for the outer planets (Uranus, Neptune, and Pluto) so only the seven visible planets are represented by the following mudras. Each mudra is named after the Sanskrit name of the planet associated with the finger, or area of hand, as follows:

Sun (Surya Mudra)

Technique: Touch the thumb tip to the ring finger tip.

Gong Playing: Steady, strong and bright. Also playing the Sun Planetary Gong.

Named after the Sun (Surya), this mudra is also called Ravi Mudra (another name for the Sun) and, like the Sun, gives revitalizing strength, excellent health, immunity, nerve strength, stability and outwardly directed energy. It is also used to strengthen potency and efficacy.

Moon (Chandra Mudra)

Technique: Join the outside of the hands together below the little finger to the base of the palms.

Gong Playing: Nurturing, variable and feminine. Also playing the Sidereal Moon or the Synodic Moon Planetary Gong.

Named after the Moon (Chandra), this mudra enhances our receptivity and intuition and brings a balance to our emotions and our thoughts as well as to our fantasies and our plans.

Mars (Mangala Mudra)

Technique: Make a fist of the hand with the thumb extended or curled inside.

Gong Playing: Aggressive, fierce and fiery. Also playing the Mars Planetary Gong.

Named after Mars (Mangala), this mudra is formed by curling the fingers into the palm and bringing the thumb outside the fist or extended up. Bringing the thumb to the base of the ring finger and making a fist around the thumb can also form it. This mudra increases courage, vitality, strength, assertion, and ability to overcome obstacles.

Mercury (Buddhi Mudra)

Technique: Touch the thumb tip to the little finger.

Gong Playing: Playful, clever and quickly. Also playing the Mercury Planetary Gong.

Named after Mercury (Buddhi) the messenger of the gods, this mudra enhances all areas of communication. It gives quickness to the mental processes, increases analytical ability, and develops intuition and psychic faculties. It is also beneficial for commerce and prosperity.

Jupiter (Gyan Mudra)

Technique: Touch the thumb tip to the index finger.

Gong Playing: Expansive, benign, and thoughtful. Also playing the Jupiter Planetary Gong.

Named for the wisdom (*gyan*) of Jupiter, this mudra is also called Chin Mudra or Jnana Mudra and is the most practiced of the planetary mudras. This mudra receives and integrates knowledge and brings calmness, expansion, and understanding. Since the dispelling of ignorance (*avidya*) is the first step toward enlightenment, this mudra is often used in meditation and pranayama practices. It is also associated with opportunity and good fortune.

Venus (Shukra Mudra)

Technique: Interlace the hands with thumbs resting side by side and not crossing. Fingers are interlaced so men press the right thumb on the mound and left little finger is on bottom. Women press the left thumb on the mound with right little finger on the bottom.

Gong Playing: Easy, sensual and spontaneous. Also playing the Venus Planetary Gong.

Named after Venus (Shukra), this mudra channels sexual energy into love and compassion and balances our sensuality.

Saturn (Shani Mudra)

Technique: Touch the thumb tip to the middle finger.

Gong Playing: Very slow, metered and methodical. Also playing the Saturn Planetary Gong.

Named after Saturn (Shani), the lord of Karma, which represents discipline, hard work, duty, responsibility, and selfless service, this mudra is used to give patience and perseverance so we can understand the lessons of time. It produces calmness, purity and humility.

BASIC PLANETARY MUDRAS

Surya Mudra (Sun)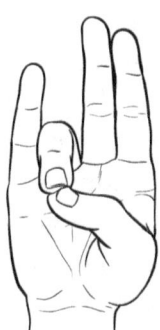

Chandra Mudra (Moon)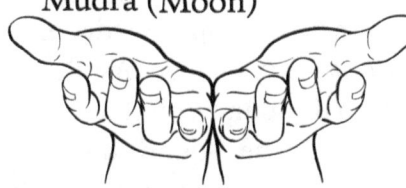

Mangala Mudra (Mars)

Budha Mudra (Mercury)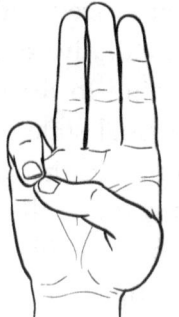

Gyan Mudra (Jupiter)

Shukra Mudra (Venus)

Shani Mudra (Saturn)

Playing the Gong for Meditation

Playing the gong for meditation is significantly different than playing the gong as an accompaniment for asanas, pranayama or relaxation. To support the state of meditation, the gong should be played to create a sound that locks and engages the mind instead of impressing or entertaining it. In other words, the cleverness or personal expression of the gong player should be subordinated to creating a neutral state of mind in the meditator.

Ideally when the gong is played for meditation, it creates a deep absorption, a vanishing of separation in the mind of the listener until there is a sense of merger between the sound of the gong and the meditative mind.

This state of absorption in sound until all else dissolves save the bliss of experience is known as Laya Yoga. As the listener becomes absorbed by the external sound of the gong, the distinction between the listener and the sound dissolves into oneness. The ability of the gong to create a sound unique to each listener so that the mind becomes entranced and stilled makes it a powerful instrument for inducing a meditative state.

With the surrender of the lower mind to the sound of the gong, the listener enters into the transcendental state of *shuniya* or a zero point of complete stillness, where inner truth can be accessed and visions spontaneously arise. In this respect, the gong is the yogi's instrument for creating a spontaneous meditative state that only requires the listener to let go and let gong.

The guidelines for playing the gong for meditation are:

- Maintain a consistency in rhythm and volume so as to not distract the listener.

- Create predictable and returning patterns in the playing, usually in the mid-area of the gong to bring balance and neutrality.

- Alternate between playing near the center of the gong and around the rim of the gong to re-direct the mind inward.

Binaural Beats and Gong Meditation

The gong is very adept at producing what are termed binaural beats, or binaural tones, by simultaneously creating one sound of two different frequencies that are heard by the listener as one tone. When this occurs, brainwave frequencies begin to align with the tones to create a state of brainwave entrainment that leads to deep meditation.

To practice creating binaural beats with the gongs, two mallets of different sizes are struck slightly out of sync in a repeated pattern to create a pulsing sound. Ideally there is only a small offset in the frequencies of the two tones created by the two mallets. This beat can also be approximated with only one mallet, by quickly striking two areas slightly off-center so that two tones blend into one sound.

An advanced practice is to meditate between two gongs. The two gongs are played in the offsetting manner as previously described for one gong so that the sound from one enters the left ear and the sound from the other enters the right ear. The gongs are played in such a close rhythm and offset that the listener distinguishes the two sounds as only one. This replicates the effect of binaural sound that is often created through the wearing of headphones.

The Gong Yoga Teacher's Practice: Meditation

When teaching Gong Yoga, the gong player should prepare by practicing meditation to awaken intuition and create a neutral space free of the ego's agenda. Ideally the meditation is done within one hour before playing the gong.

The meditation can consist of simple pranayamas, recitation of mantras, or performing asanas. Yoga sets (kriyas) and meditations that work on the fifth and sixth chakras are particularly effective in preparing the teacher to play the gong. Here are examples of simple and short meditations that activate the flow of prana through the higher chakras (4, 5, 6, and 7) before playing the gong:

Meditation to Open the Heart and Play with Compassion

Sit in a comfortable meditative posture. Block the right nostril with the thumb or finger of the right hand. Inhale smoothly and fully through the left nostril only. Exhale for an equal length of tie through the pursed lips. The left hand can rest on the center of the chest or heart chakra. After 5 minutes, relax the hands and breath. Meditate for 2 more minutes on the natural flow of the breath

Meditation to Activate the Throat Chakra

Sit in a comfortable meditative posture. Interlace the fingers so that the palms face down and held slight out from the heart. The thumbs relax open and point back to the body.

Inhale and move the interlaced hands quickly up to the brow point or third eye. Exhale and move them quickly down to the heart again, passing back and forth over the throat chakra. Make the movement rapid, almost once per second, so the breath becomes almost like the Breath of Fire (Agni Pran).

After 3 minutes, inhale to the level of the third eye, retain the breath for 20 seconds and pull the hands. Exhale and relax.

Meditation to Awaken Intuition and Third Eye

Sit in a comfortable meditative posture. Focus at the two nostrils and the third eye (brow point). Imagine inhaling only through the left nostril and up to the brow point. Then imagine exhaling only through the right nostril. Now inhale through the right nostril to the brown point and exhale back down through the left nostril. Switch sides and continue back and forth, breathing through alternate nostrils without using the fingers, for 3 to 7 minutes or longer.

Meditation to Open the Crown Chakra

Sit in a meditative posture. Interlace the hands and press them on top of the head. Press the tongue against the roof of the mouth. Roll the eyes up as if to look through the top of the head. Begin Breath of Fire and continue for 5 minutes. Inhale, hold, press the hands down and the tongue up. Exhale and release the hands and tongue.

Ritual and the Gong: Playing for the Bliss Body

In using the kosha model in the practice of Gong Yoga, the bliss body or the anandamaya kosha, is accessed through the technique of ritual. Along with mantras, the practice of ritual is one of the oldest practices of yoga as described in the Rg Veda, and even today in India and beyond, it is the fire rituals and the pujas (ceremonies) that still play an important part in the spiritual evolution of the yogi and yogini. Indeed, the common feature among every spiritual tradition and yoga practice is the performance of ritual, and the practice of Gong Yoga lends itself easily to using this technique to experience the final and fifth layer of existence, the anandamaya kosha.

The word ritual comes from the Latin *ritus* that means to fit together. In the practice of yoga, the ritual is what fits or connects together the finite with infinite, the form with the formless, and the transient with the eternal. Ritual is a gesture or action performed in the material world of the five elements that connects us to the transcendent plane of spirit. Ritual is the relationship we create between the Individual Self with the Universal Self, and the gong is uniquely suited to performing this connection.

The Gong and Its Role in Rituals

The primary function of the gong across all cultures was to mark and create a ritual. The gong has been involved in every kind of human activity, from the earthly to the ethereal. In Buddhist monasteries, gongs call the attention of the gods. In ancient Greece, they opened the realm of the dead. In Borneo, they are beaten to frighten away storms. In Ceram, gongs are given as wedding gifts. In Assam, they are used as funeral pyres. During war, gongs intimidate enemies and gather troops. In peace, they celebrate festivals and accompany dances. Even the ritual of coming to a formal meal was announced by the dinner gong in the early twentieth century.

The gong has played an important role in ceremonies, rituals, and inner journeys among all the world's peoples. Deaths, births, marriages, and initiations were all accompanied by the sounding of the gong. For thousands of years, across all civilizations, all who hear it instinctively recognize the power of the gong to announce or mark a time of transition, of new beginnings or final endings. When the gong is played, the body, mind and spirit change through this timeless ritual and ethereal sound.

The gong may be used alone to create the experience of ritual and access the anandamaya kosha in a yoga class. The opening of the class with one or more strikes of the gong, or the closing of the class by simply sounding the gong, can signify the ritual transition betwwen profane and sacred space. When the gong is played consistently this way to begin and/or to end a Gong Yoga practice, it signals to the practitioner that a ritual is occurring that is beyond ordinary consciousness.

In addition to these simple opening and closing rituals,, the gong player may create their own ways to connect their energy to the energy of the gong and the higher self. Simply bowing the head, touching the heart, or giving a silent blessing can be enough to change from the mundane to the sacred work of playing the gong.

The Five Elements and Performance of Rituals

Rituals are constructed from elemental materials, or the *mahabhuta tattvas* of earth, water, fire, air and ether. By working with these material elements, we can construct rituals that take us beyond our earthly sensibilities. These physical elements of ritual comprise the most ancient language that speaks to everyone and may be represented in several ways.

Element (Tattva)	Represented By:
Earth (Prithvi)	Sacred stones, flowers, statues, precious metals, incense
Water (Jala)	Blessed water, blood, wine, reproductive fluids, elixirs
Fire (Agni)	Bonfires, candles, open flames, lights, sun, illumined objects
Air (Vayu)	Singing, prayer, mantra, feathers, the breath, wind instruments
Ether (Akash)	Gongs, bells, drums, chimes, stringed instruments

An elaborate gong ritual can be constructed by using some or all five of these fundamental elements. For example, a Gong Yoga session may be introduced by the lighting of incense (*prithvi*), the sprinkling of purified water (*jala*), the lighting of a candle (*agni*), the repetition of a mantra (*vayu*), and the strike of the gong (*akash*). When the gong is used in a ritual with other elements, it should always be the initiating and/or terminating element as all things come from ether (*akash*) and return to ether.

The Gong Yoga Teacher's Practice: Ritual

The Gong Yoga teacher may incorporate ritual into the class in several ways. A simple ritual is to cover the gong at the end of a playing session (and consequently uncovering it at the beginning). The covering is a sign of respect for the hidden mysteries of the gong, acknowledging its ability to reveal what is hidden from us when it is unhidden by the player. Practically, the covering of the gong also prevents the electrostatic attraction of dust and particulates that can affect the sound of the gong and eventually harm its surface.

Another pragmatic ritual is the periodic cleaning of the gong with a soft cloth and vinegar and water, or an appropriate cleaning solution. Cleansing practices of all types, from bathing to fasting, figure prominently in many rituals and spiritual practices, and the cleaning of the gong reminds us of the purity we are to bring to our playing. Again in a practical manner, cleaning the gong surface preserves the purity and crispness of the sound when it is played.

A more esoteric clearing of the gong can be done through the ritual application of an essential oil, preferably sandalwood or essence of amber. Care must be taken that the oil is very, very lightly applied or rubbed onto a cloth and then on to the surface of the gong; otherwise, the surface will become oily and hold onto dust and eventually affect the mallet as well. The idea is to subtly bring the clarifying fragrance into the aura of the gong and not massage the oil into it. Sandalwood has been used for centuries to open the higher chakras and cleanse the aura.

Some players have a ritual of asking the gong to guide them through their playing and teaching, or simply making an offering of their playing to a higher entity. Other players may wear certain clothing, sacred malas or jewelry, or carry sacred objects on their person when playing the gong.

The purpose of all these rituals is simply to connect the gong player to a higher guidance that exists beyond the teacher's ego and human agenda.

Opening Mantra as Ritual

One of the most significant and powerful rituals is to use an opening or centering mantra before the gong is played in order to attune the player to the power of the sound of the gong. This linkage between the player and the gong creates the intuitive relationship that allows the gong to play the player as well as the player to play the gong.

In Kundalini Yoga, the specific linkage between the gong player and the gong is made through a series of three mantras. Each of the following mantras is repeated silently or chanted before the gong is played.

AD GUREY NAMEH
JUGAD GUREY NAMEH
SAT GURU NAMEH
SIRI GURU DEV A NAMEH

ONG NAMO GURU DEV NAMO

AD SUCH JUGAD SUCH HAIBHEE SUCH
NANAK HOSEE BHEE SUCH

The first mantra brings you before the timeless teacher, to lay aside your ego, and to allow the wisdom through all the ages to guide you, and is translated as follows:

AD GUREY NAMEH
(I call upon the teacher who exists at the Beginning)
JUGAD GUREY NAMEH
(I call upon the teacher who teaches through all times)
SAT GUREY NAMEH
(I call upon the teacher who teaches from the Truth)
SIRI GURU DEV A NAMEH
(I call upon the unseen subtle teacher of all)

The second mantra links to the creative energy of the universe, the feminine creative power that rules music and all forms of expression, the sound of ONG, of creation itself:

ONG NAMO
(I call upon the Infinite Creative Energy)
GURU DEV NAMO
(I call upon the divine transcendent teacher)

The third mantra takes the mind to the point where sound exists in the eternal moment of truth, beyond polarities and indistinguishable from the sound and the producer of the sound.

AD SUCH
(The truth before all beginnings)
JUGAD SUCH
(The truth through all ages)
HAIBHEE SUCH
(The truth at this moment)
NANAK HOSEE BHEE SUCH
(The truth that is ever true)

Once these mantras are used with the proper intention, the gong player plays what is needed at the present moment and not from the ego of a performer. The karma of the playing becomes dharma and elevates both the player and the listener.

Mantras from other spiritual and yogic traditions may also be used as part of the ritual opening. For example, an offering and mantra may be given to Saraswati, the Vedic goddess of music, arts and knowledge. Honey is the traditional ingredient offered to this goddess of music on the altar. This frequently used mantra may also be used to invoke the energy of Sarawsati before playing the gong:

OM AING SARASWATYE NAMAH OM

The seed or bija mantra **AING** can also be repeated by itself to invoke the energy of the goddess of music, knowledge, sound and arts.

Another useful energy to invoke is that of Ganesha, the deity that removes all blocks and brings us knowledge of the divine. Two simple and powerful Ganesha mantras are:

OM GAM GANAPATAYE NAMAH

OM SHRI GANESHAYA NAMAH

Finally, simply invoking the name of your teacher or that feeling which represents the divine to you is a most effective ritual to open the channel from the player to the infinite.

Relaxation and the Gong: Playing for Integration

As we complete the journey through the five koshas using the techniques of asana, pranayama, mantra, meditation and ritual with the gong, we finish the integration of these energy bodies into wholeness through the experience of relaxation.

Experiencing the gong during relaxation at the end of a yoga class is perhaps one of the most common ways people encounter the healing and transformational sound of the gong. Yet without adequate preparation and awareness on the part of the student, as well as intentionality and understanding by the teacher, the gong relaxation can become a low energy or *tamasic* experience, much like a nap or a warm bath.

While listening to the gong while napping or resting in a semi-conscious state is enjoyable, the opportunity that a well-done relaxation to the gong can provide is missed. There are preparations and practices, as well as playing techniques by the teacher, to create the experience of a profound gong relaxation.

The basic guidelines for Gong Yoga relaxation are: 1) Yoga practices are done prior to relaxation; 2) Preparation for the relaxation is conducted by the teacher; 3) The gong is consciously played by the teacher to induce and maximize the experience of relaxation; 4) The relaxation is done in a state of awareness with a pure and light (*sattvic*) quality.

Yoga Practices for Relaxation

Most uncomfortable experiences that people may have with the gong usually occur because the gong is not played in a yogic environment and participants are not ready to receive the sound.

For the most part, almost any yoga class with an appropriate balance of postures and breath work will create a receptive state for gong relaxation. It is not necessary that the class itself be a Gong Yoga class. It is only required that the practices in the yoga class be authentic or follow a specific style or recognized lineage.

If other techniques and practices are borrowed from non-yogic traditions or created by the teacher, the results may be unpredictable. Remember that you are creating Gong Yoga relaxation, and while a relaxation that occurs after a mix of various physical, mental or emotional practices can be healing and beneficial, it also poses uncertain outcomes. You certainly can use other modalities with the gong as therapy, **if you are a skilled practitioner in that modality.** The gong is a powerful instrument for transformation so staying within the yoga tradition provides you, as a yoga teacher, a tested method in which to work.

Preparation for Relaxation

The preparation for gong relaxation follows a sequence of yoga practices that address the physical, energetic and emotional bodies by using the techniques of asana, pranayama, and visualization.

The Physical Environment

The place for the gong relaxation should reduce sensory stimulation as much as possible. Dimmed lights or covering the eyes is important as sight increases the response of the sympathetic nervous system that takes us into action. The body may be covered lightly to reduce unwanted tactile stimulation, such as air circulation, and to increase the body temperature that precedes a relaxed state. Smell is a potent and sometimes overlooked stimulator and distractor; especially food odors and scents that can arouse distracting memories and emotions.

While the sound of the gong can mask outside sounds, reducing ambient noise is important and it may be helpful to lightly cover the ears or top of the head, or turn the sound of the heating or air conditioning systems off. The gong will still be effective even if the ears are lightly covered and the covered filtered sound can reduce anxiety that some people may have regarding the powerful sound of the gong. Even with the ears covered, the gong will be able to accomplish its work.

Be aware that all hearing aid devices must be turned off before the gong is played. As much as possible, the physical environment should facilitate sensory withdrawal, or *pratyahara*, in order to maximize the effect of the sound of the gong.

Preparing the Physical Body

Ideally asanas or *kriyas* (sequences of exercise with yoga techniques) are done to release tension and prepare the body for relaxation. The asanas immediately preceding relaxation should be slow and cooling (*langhana*). The asanas do not have to be elaborate or lengthy; simple head turns or neck rolls, flexing the ankles or turning the hands, drawing the knees into the chest while on the back, all enhance the ability of the body to relax.

Relaxation is optimally done in a supine position, using variations of *savasana*, or corpse pose. In environments where lying down is not an option, relaxation can be done seated in a chair.

While the classic corpse pose is done on the back with the hands and arms slightly apart, and palms turned upward, the palms can be turned down to accommodate the shoulders and the knees can be bent or supported under the knees to aid the lower back. The pose can also be done lying on one side (preferably the left side) with the knees pulled up and the head supported on the arm or thin cushion.

If the primary purpose of the gong playing is to create deep physical relaxation, then the feet should be pointed toward the gong in order to ground the body. If the intention is to dissociate the ethereal or astral body from the physical body during relaxation to create a sense of lightness or release, then the head may be pointed toward the gong. For those who are easily spaced out, or susceptible to vata derangement, then the top of the head can be covered or wrapped with a blanket. A light cushion or eye pillow over the eyes and forehead can be beneficial for inducing relaxation.

Preparing the Energy Body

Working with the breath through breathing practices is the most effective way to prepare the energetic or subtle body for gong relaxation. The breathing practices may be done before or during the relaxation. Breathing practices immediately before relaxation should be cooling (*langhana*) or balancing (*samana*) in effect.

Some ideal pranayamas to induce relaxation are:

- Breathing through the left nostril only
- Inhaling left, exhaling right
- Alternate nostril breathing
- Sitali (tongue extended) breathing
- Humming Bee breath

When entering relaxation on the back, attention can be directed to an easy diaphragmatic breath, focusing on the rise and fall of the stomach or diaphragm, or upon a full body breath, inhaling from the feet to the crown of the head and exhaling from crown to feet. A simple way to create relaxation is to gently extend the length of the exhalation so it becomes twice as long as the inhalation.

A more passive relaxation breath is to begin relaxing on the right side of the body for 3-5 minutes and that will gently shift the dominant breathing pattern to the left nostril and activate the parasympathetic nervous system. After a few minutes roll onto the back or remain on the right side if more comfortable.

Preparing the Emotional Body

The emotional body can be prepared for gong relaxation through visualizations, affirmations, and silent mantra.

The teacher may repeat one or more of the following affirmations out loud, one to three times, and then have the student repeat the affirmation silently. Depending upon the energetic or emotional state of the practitioner, or the intention for the relaxation, affirmations may be selected according to which chakra or major emotional issue is being addressed as the following table illustrates.

CHAKRA	AFFIRMATIONS
FIRST Muladhara	I am safe. I am secure. I am grounded. I am prosperous. I am here.
SECOND Svadhisthana	I am connected. I am spontaneous. I am worthy. I am creative. I am deserving.
THIRD Manipura	I am able. I am strong. I am willful. I am self-sufficient. I am determined.
FOURTH Anahata	I am compassionate. I am neutral. I am willing. I am balanced. I am accepting.
FIFTH Vishuddha	I am truthful. I am clear. I am effective. I am receptive. I am expressive.
SIXTH Ajna	I am perceptive. I am intuitive. I am focused. I am guided. I am ready.
SEVENTH Sahasrara	I am aware. I am trusting. I am divine. I am aligned. I am One.

Playing the Gong for Relaxation

Generally, the gong should be played for a minimum of 7 minutes to create deep relaxation and to balance the sympathetic and parasympathetic nervous systems.

Unlike playing the gong for meditation and pranayama in which consistent patterns are followed to induce concentration and focus, playing the gong for relaxation requires the player to engage the listener in a guiding and sometimes challenging manner to create a release of tension and removal of blocks that inhibit relaxation.

A classic relaxation technique in therapy and yoga is progressive muscle relaxation, or PMR, in which areas of the body are first contracted and then relaxed in order to create an awareness of the residual tension and stress that may be inherent (and hidden) in the body of the practitioner. In other words, pressure is consciously applied and the consciously released, giving the practitioner control over the physically stressed areas in the body.

While effective for many people, PMR with contraction can cause some people to feel more tension and become more stressed. Fortunately, the gong can be played in such a way that pressure can be applied through sound and then released through sound rather than the physical contraction that can create discomfort. More importantly, the gong goes beyond dealing with the simple muscular tension, which is symptomatic and not causative of stress, and addresses the root cause of stress by rebalancing the nervous system.

Stress and the inability to relax is fundamentally experienced as a result of the sympathetic nervous system (the fight or flight response) being overactive and the parasympathetic nervous system (which supports relaxation) being unable to turn back on.

The gong works through the sympathetic and parasympathetic nervous systems to create deep relaxation through playing sequences that are termed build and release cycles.

Build and Release Cycles for Gong Relaxation

Simply put, a build and release cycle occurs when the gong is played in a repetitive pattern, often with an increase in rhythm, volume, or both, in order to create an expectancy or inner tension in the mind of the listener that continues to build and build until a release from the tension is delivered through a culmination or completion of the building pattern.

An apt comparison is the sexual tension that builds to a heightened intensity and then climatically releases through orgasm, resulting in relaxation and a sense of completion.

For example, a simple build and release cycle is to repeatedly strike one point on the gong, gradually building its rhythm or volume to a point of intensity, and then breaking the playing pattern with a single (or multiple) strike that releases the mind and nervous system of the listener.

The building of the sound through repeated patterns over time builds an expectancy and even desire in the listener for the pattern to be released. This has the same effect of the sympathetic nervous system (the desire to break away from the pattern) that muscular contraction has on the physical body.

When the release strike breaks the pattern, the sympathetic nervous system can shut down and the parasympathetic nervous system of relaxation can now assert itself. To effectively retrain the listener to shut off the sympathetic nervous system and turn on the parasympathetic response often requires three build and release cycles be done during the gong relaxation.

While the loud volume or fast rhythm of the gong during these building cycles may seem counterintuitive to inducing deep relaxation, they serve the same function as applying stressors (such as muscle contraction) in a conscious manner in order to create deep release when the stressors are removed.

The Gong and Yoga Nidra

One of the most profound ways to create relaxation with the gong is through a guided process known as Yoga Nidra, or yogic sleep. Yoga Nidra induces deep relaxation, heightens awareness, enables self-diagnosis, integrates changes, and accelerates healing. It is a powerful tool for therapeutic change that is accomplished over an extended (30 to 60 minute) relaxation period.

The practice of Yoga Nidra purifies the deep impressions of the individual's *samskaras*, the driving and often hidden karmic forces behind many of our actions and conditions. Essentially, the state of Yoga Nidra gives access to the mind that is underneath our normal processing, fantasizing and imagining consciousness. It is an excellent tool for attenuating and eliminating habit patterns that are the root causes of physical and psychological problems that manifest in long-term stress and an inability to relax.

While Yoga Nidra can be practiced in many ways, there is a standard sequence for a Gong Yoga Nidra relaxation session. Notice how this sequence follows the kosha model to create a journey of holistic healing through all five layers of existence.

Opening the Space – At the beginning of a Yoga Nidra practice, the participants relax on the back. Blankets or yoga props may be used to keep the body comfortably still. Give a reminder to remain awake and aware in order to receive the full benefits of the practice, and to simply follow the teacher's voice and listen to the sound of the gong.

The teacher opens the space by gently striking the gong three times. In the ensuing silence, the teacher asks the participants to select a precise, clear and positive intention or resolve for the session. This positive resolve is known as a *sankalpa*. The Sanskrit word means a resolution or determination, and is a basic tool in initiating a yogic healing process to awaken innate healing energies. A typical sankalpa might be, "I experience radiant health," or "I am free of all pain." The sankalpa should be in the present tense as if it has already occurred. Ask them to silently repeat it to themselves, and then strike the gong once and announce, *"The practice of Yoga Nidra has begun."*

Body Awareness - While in a state of relaxation after setting the intention, the teacher directs the participant's awareness to the different areas of the body. By rotating the participant's awareness through all areas of the body in a systematic fashion, a body-mind state is created that begins the process of integration. Generally, a specific sequence is used to direct body awareness, beginning with the right hand, the right side, moving to the left side, to the back of the body, to the front of the body, the head, face, and back down to the legs. The example given later in the sample script may be followed. During this segment, the gong is usually not played. This practice awakens the anamaya kosha.

Breath Awareness – After the rotation of consciousness, an awareness of the breath is established, either through counting or breathing into different areas or points on the body. This awakens the flow of prana and energy to every cell in the body. The example given later in the sample script may be followed. The gong may be optionally played during this segment to direct the inhale and exhale or retention or suspension of the breath. This practice awakens the pranamaya kosha.

Sensation Awareness – Now feelings and emotions are awakened, experienced, and removed through a directed focusing on pairs of opposites, such as hot and cold, joy and sadness, love and fear, light and dark. This contrasting of opposites through words or imagery allows for emotional balancing and relaxation and integration of the brain hemispheres. The example given later in the sample script may be followed. During this segment, the gong is not played. This practice awakens the manamaya kosha.

Guided Meditation - This stage of Yoga Nidra uses visualizations by the participant based upon suggestions from the instructor. The guided visualization awakens the third eye of the participant and begins the inner journey into the subconscious. This process develops concentration and dissolves the distinctions between the conscious and unconscious mind, allowing it to completely relax. The teacher can create or use a guided visualization of their own or may use the example script given later. During this segment, the gong may be played to underscore or emphasize a particular visual image as long as it does not overwhelm the participant's ability to follow the teacher's visualizations. This practice awakens the vijnanamaya kosha.

Relaxation and Integrations - The stage of Yoga Nidra allows the participant to experience the bliss body or anandamaya kosha through the extended playing of the gong. In this stage, the gong is played intuitively for 7 to 31 minutes. More than one gong or gong player may participate. Three or more build and release cycles may be included in the session, as well as periods of near silence. At the end of this segment, there should be several distinctive gong strikes to signal the ending, and then allow for one minute of total silence.

Closing the Space - The participants are brought back into the body by directing the breath consciously in and out several times. The gong is no longer played. Before they move their body, the teacher reminds the participants of their original intention, or sankalpa, from the beginning of the session. They are asked to mentally repeat their intention three times.

The session ends with the participants gently moving, stretching. And slowly coming up to a seated posture. Close the session with a gong strike, a chanted mantra, a prayer or a blessing. If they are with others, have them turn to someone and discuss their experience. If they are alone, make yourself available as a sounding board for their experience. Do not judge or direct the conversation. Simply affirm what you are hearing.

Within these guidelines, there is much flexibility in constructing a Gong Yoga Nidra session, and ideas can be garnered from various books and examples of Yoga Nidra practices. You can also write your own scripts and experiment with different images and guided visualizations. Two example scripts follow.

Gong Yoga Nidra: Integration through Sound

This Gong Yoga Nidra script incorporates the sound of the gong as an integral part of the narrative visualization. As you read the script, please modify it for your speaking and teaching style.

It is not uncommon for some people to fall asleep during the practice. To encourage them to stay awake and be present to receive the full benefits of the practice, keep the voice strong and directed. You may find it easier to be seated as you read the script and use a floor stand for the gong so it can be easily played without getting up and down.

A Yoga Nidra session often takes a little longer than you might expect as you do not wish to rush the experience and you will need to provide pauses for integration.

(1) Opening the Space

Relax comfortably on your back. Feel and connect to the easy flow of your breath. (Silent pause)

(The gong is struck 3 times softly.)

Allow a conscious intention to arise in your mind for this session of Yoga Nidra. It should be a short, positive affirmation in the present moment, such as "I am healed in every cell of my body" or "I am relaxed with each breath I take." Allow the intention to enter your consciousness and then silently repeat it three times to yourself. (Silent pause)

(The gong is struck one time.)

The practice of Yoga Nidra now begins. Relax deeply but remain awake and aware. Completely relax and follow the sound of my voice. Repeat to yourself, "I will remain awake. I will remain aware. I will fully experience this moment."

(Silent pause. The gong is struck one time.)

(2) Body Awareness

Now let you awareness quickly move to each area of the body that I name. Simply take your awareness there and then move immediately to the next area. (Silent pause. Then speak slowly.)

Right hand ... right palm ... right wrist ... lower right arm ... elbow ... upper arm ... right shoulder ... right armpit ... right side of body ... right waist ... right hip ... right thigh ... kneecap ... calf muscle ... right ankle ... right heel ... top of right foot ... bottom of foot.

Left hand ... left palm ... left wrist ... lower left arm ... elbow ... upper arm ... left shoulder ... left armpit ... left side of body ... left waist ... left hip ... left thigh ... kneecap ... calf muscle ... left ankle ... left heel ... top of left foot ... bottom of foot.

Top of head ... forehead ... right eyebrow ... left eyebrow ... right eyelid ... left eyelid ... right eye ... left eye ... right nostril ... left nostril ... right cheek ... left cheek ... upper lip ... lower lip ... chin ... jaw... throat ... right chest ... left chest ... navel ... upper abdomen ... lower abdomen ... right thigh ... left thigh ... right knee ... left knee ... right calf muscle ... left calf muscle ... right ankle ... left ankle ... right foot ... left foot.

Whole right leg ... whole left leg ... both legs together ... whole right arm ... whole left arm ... both arms together ... whole of the head together ... whole of the back together ... whole of the front together ... the whole body together ... the whole body together ... the whole body together.

(Silent pause. The gong is struck one time.)

(3) Breath Awareness

Now bring your awareness to your breath. Become aware of the movement of the breath. Feel the breath as it enters the nostrils. Feel the breath as it leaves the nostrils. Feel the movement of the breath throughout the body. Feel the rise and fall of the diaphragm with each inhale and each exhale. (Silent pause)

Now focus on the breath entering and leaving at the tip of the nose. Feel the breath entering and leaving the nostrils. Sense the movement of the breath moving from the tip of the nose to the third eye point above the eyebrows. Allow the breath to move back and forth between the tip of the nose and the third eye. Inhale up to the third eye. Exhale down to the tip. Feel the breath travel from the nose to the brow point and from the brow point to the nose. (Silent pause)

Now begin to count the breaths as you inhale from the tip of the nose to the third eye and exhale down from the third eye to the tip of the nose. Count backwards silently from thirty, as follows: Inhaling Thirty, Exhaling Thirty. Inhaling Twenty-nine, Exhaling Twenty-nine. Inhaling Twenty-eight, Exhaling Twenty-eight. Keep counting backwards. If you lose count, start over again at Thirty and count each breath as it moves in and out. Breathe consciously and slowly. Feel the breath moving in and out with each count.

(Silent pause for 2-3 minutes. The gong is struck one time.)

(4) Sensation Awareness

Now let your breath and counting relax. Continue to let your awareness rest on the easy flow of your breath. Remain awake and aware. Remain awake and aware, as I name objects and you should try to visualize them on the levels of feeling, awareness, emotion and imagination as best you can.

(Silent Pause)

You should jump your mind from image to image, not concentrating on any one image, but keep moving and allow all sensations and feelings to quickly arise and disappear.

(Silent pause. The gong is struck one time. Then the following images are spoken.)

Cold winter day... Cold winter day

Leafless tree in the sun ... Leafless tree in the sun

Frightened dog barking ... Frightened dog barking

Black stones in a clear stream... Black stones in a clear stream

Old woman crying ... Old woman crying

Knife in an empty glass ... Knife in an empty glass

Apple pie baking ... Apple pie baking

Child in an empty room... Child in an empty room

Ashes on a wooden floor ... Ashes on a wooden floor

Wind banging door... Wind banging door

Smiling Buddha ... Smiling Buddha

Broken window in the rain... Broken window in the rain

Kittens nursing with claws... Kittens nursing with claws

White roses blooming ... White roses blooming

Tombstone covered in blood... Tombstone covered in blood

Restless tiger in a cage... Restless tiger in a cage

Snowflakes falling on fire... Snowflakes falling on fire

Yogi in a cave ... Yogi in a cave

Bells ringing on a rope... Bells ringing on a rope

Mother holding sleeping child ... Mother holding sleeping child

Lying in a warm bath ...Lying in a warm bath

A torn and patched coat ... A torn and patched coat

Incense burning on an altar... Incense burning on an altar

Field of sunflowers ... Field of sunflowers

Full moon rising ... Full moon rising

(Silent pause. The gong is struck one time.)

(5) Guided Meditation

Let your eyes relax and turn upward. Let your eyes relax upward. Let your awareness take you on an inner journey. Go deeper and deeper inside. Become a witness of yourself. Become a watcher of the story that unfolds within you. Become the observer beyond time and space. (Silent pause)

See yourself standing on the beach of an infinite ocean, calm and quiet, as the gentle waves roll up to your feet. Feel the wet sand beneath you and the warmth of the sun upon you. Smell the salt in the wind and see the birds flying over the water. Feel the cooling wind on your skin. Listen to the sound of the waves, and hear the birds calling. Listen and hear. Listen and hear. And from the distance, hear the sound of a gong from far away.

(The gong is struck softly and allowed to fade completely away.)

As you turn from the ocean toward the sound of the gong, you see a cool green jungle. From the palm tress, a path leads from the beach and disappears into the jungle. From deep within the jungle, you hear the gong again, like a softly beating heart.

(The gong is played with a heart beat rhythm and fades away.)

You take the path into the jungle and walk toward the sound of the distant gong. With each step, the sound of the gong grows and calls you to come closer.

(The gong is played slightly louder and fades away.)

You come to a clearing in the jungle and before you is a magnificent gong hanging between two trees. There is no one around, and as you walk toward the gong the sound grows and swells and surrounds you.

(The gong is played with a strong rhythm and then with a single strong strike, it fades completely away.)

Standing in front of the gong, you close your eyes in gratitude. As you open your eyes, you see your reflection on the shinning surface of the gong, like a mirror, looking back at you.

The reflection in the gong is the image of the person you are becoming. It is your most divine self, your most radiant being, your most loving nature, that looks back at you, holding you in infinite compassion and acceptance. See the reflection, smiling at you, accepting you and reminding you that the person that is looking and the person that is reflected are both the same, forever one, forever eternal, and completely perfect in this moment.

(Silent pause.)

(6) Relaxation and Integration

The gong is played for 7 to 15 minutes and then lasting silence.

(7) Closing the Space

Inhale gently and fully. Exhale. Let your breath return to your conscious control. Inhaling and exhaling. (Pause) *Now remember your intention and affirmation you made at the beginning of relaxation. Repeat the affirmation silently three times. Let it be so. Now deepen the breath and begin to move the fingers and toes. Circle the hands around the wrists and the feet around the ankles. Reverse the circles. Please inhale the arms over the head and stretch in both directions. Bring the hands together over the heart and rub the palms together and rub the feet together. Bring your knees into you chest and rock side to side and then roll over to one side. Slowly bring yourself up to sitting.* (A mantra can be chanted to close the session or simply hold in silence.) *The practice of Yoga Nidra has now ended.* (Single gong strike.)

Participants should talk and share their experiences to process and integrate the profound changes of this practice and take their time to re-enter the world from this sacred space.

Gong Yoga Nidra to Balance the Chakras

This Gong Yoga Nidra script uses simple supported asanas that may be done on the back during the guided meditation. While most Yoga Nidra sessions do not use movement, in this case the postures create a deeper opening into the journey through the chakras. Please modify for your speaking and teaching style.

(1) **Opening the Space** – Same as previous session.

(2) **Body Awareness** – Same as previous session.

(3) **Breath Awareness** – Same as previous session, or use the Point-to-Point breathing exercise or other breathing exercises that may be done on the back.

(4) **Sensation Awareness** – Same as previous session or create your own imagery and symbols to access the unconscious mind.

(5) **Guided Meditation**

Let your awareness move to the base of your spine. Breathe into that space and feel the sensations around the base of the spine. Let the breath amplify all sensations and feelings around the base of the spine. Is there a sense of contraction or expansion ... Lightness or heaviness ... a color or an image? Let the breath move to that area of your body. Now draw the knees into the chest with the hands and hold the knees down. Focus and breathe into the base of the spine.

(The gong is played for the first chakra, near the bottom of the gong while the posture is held for 1 to 2 minutes. Then silence.)

Now release the posture and relax into the breath. Breathe into the hips and pelvic area. Let the breath amplify all sensations and feelings around the pelvic area. Is there a sense of contraction or expansion ... Lightness or heaviness ... a color or an image? Let the breath move freely. Now bring the soles of the feet together and pull the heels up so that the knees fall open to the sides, like an open butterfly. Focus and breathe into pelvic area.

(The gong is played for the second chakra, above the bottom of the gong, for 1 to 2 minutes. Then the gong is silenced.)

Now release the posture and relax into the breath. Begin to breathe into the area around the navel point and solar plexus. Let the breath amplify all sensations and feelings around the abdomen area. Connect to the rise and fall of the diaphragm. Is there a sense of contraction or expansion … Lightness or heaviness … a color or an image? Let the breath move to that area of your body. Now slide the hands under the hips palms down and pull the knees into the chest. Gradually extend your legs out between 6 inches (15 centimeters) and three feet (one meter) above the ground. Bend the knees if you need to protect you back, but keep the feet off the floor. Focus and breathe into navel point area. Keep the abdominal muscles engaged.

(The gong is played for the third chakra, right below the center of the gong, for 1 to 2 minutes while the posture is held. Then the gong is silenced.)

Now lower the legs and relax into the breath. Begin to breathe into the area around the heart. Breathe into the heart and breathe out from the heart. Let the breath open the heart area. Let the breath amplify all sensations and feelings around the heart area. Connect to the breath moving in and out of the heart. Is there a sense of contraction or expansion … Lightness or heaviness … a color or an image? Let the breath move to that area of your body. Now begin to press the heart upward through the ribcage. Keep the back on the floor but maintain a constant upward pressure on the heart as if you could push it up, as if a string was lifting the chest and heart upward. Keep the upward pressure and breathe; breathe into the heart.

(The gong is played for the fourth chakra, right above the center of the gong, for 1 to 2 minutes. Then the gong is silenced.)

Now relax the chest, relax the heart, and release all the pressure around the heart center. Breathe and relax. Begin to breathe into the area around the throat. Breathe into the throat and hear the sound of the breath in the throat. Breathe in and out from the throat and let the breath open the throat area. Let the breath amplify all sensations and feelings around the throat. Connect to the breath moving in and out of the throat. Is there a sense of contraction or expansion ... Lightness or heaviness ... a color or an image? Let the breath move to that area of your body. Now slide the hands under the hips again, palms down, and gently lift the head and bring the top or the back of the head on the floor so the neck is comfortably arched and the throat is opened. If the neck is uncomfortable, release the head onto the floor and continue hearing the sound of the breath in the throat

(The gong is played for the fifth chakra, between the center of the gong and the rim, for 1 to 2 minutes. Then it is silenced.)

Now relax the head and neck and gently rock the head side to side along the floor. Swallow and release any tension Relax the neck, and release all the pressure around the throat center. Breathe and relax. Begin to breathe into the area above and between the eyebrows. Draw the breath into the brow point, as if the breath can enter and leave through the third eye. Imagine the brow point as the lens of a camera opening to receive the breath into the body, and breathe in and out through the third eye. Imagine the breath as a shaft of light that enters the body as you inhale and then projects from the third eye you exhale. Let the breath amplify all sensations and feelings around the third eye. Connect to the breath moving in and out of the brow point. Is there a sense of contraction or expansion ... Lightness or heaviness ... a color or an image? Let the breath move to that area of your body. See any images, any colors, or any symbols that might appear on the screen of your third eye. Now roll the eyes strongly up to the third eye point and hold the inner gaze steadily with focus and intention. Keep the eyes locked upward and inward, behind the root of the nose and back into the brain.

(The gong is played for the sixth chakra, below the top rim for 1 to 2 minutes. Then the gong is silenced.)

Now relax the gaze and the eyes. Let the eyes completely relax. Breathe and relax. Begin to breathe into the area at the top of the head. Take the breath all the way up to the crown of the head. Feel the breath entering the top of the head as you inhale and feel the breath leaving through the top of the head as you exhale. Breateh in and out from the top of the head, gradually extending the breath above the head, a few inches, a few inches more, and finally as far as the mind can project, drawing the breath in from infinity and out from infinity. Sense the vastness beyond the physical body, feel the expansion of self above time and space. Now press the tongue against the roof of the mouth and roll the eyes upward as if you could look through the top of the head.

(The gong is played for the seventh chakra, at the edge of rim near the top of the gong with light upward expansive strikes. Finally the gong is played all along the rim, starting from the top and sweeping around to the bottom and back to the top is several circles of increasing rhythm the top rim for 1 to 2 minutes while the posture is held. Then the gong is silenced.)

Now relax the eyes, relax the tongue, relax the breath, and relax the whole body. Breathe and relax. Feel the wholeness of the body. Feel the whole body together. Breathe through the whole body, from the soles of the feet to the crown of the head. Let the breath move through all the chakras, along the spine, along the whole body. And relax... relax... relax.

(6) **Relaxation and Integration**

The gong is played along the axis of the chakras, from bottom to top and top to bottom, for 7 minutes and then fades to a lasting silence.

(7) **Closing the Space** – Same as previous session.

The Gong and Styles of Yoga

The gong can be easily integrated into all the Western styles of yoga, which tend mostly to be variations on the Hatha and Kundalini Yoga traditions.

Outside of Hatha and Kundalini traditions, which are further described in this chapter, the gong can be prominently used in the practices of Laya Yoga, Mantra Yoga, Raja Yoga, and Nada Yoga. Given the right circumstances, the gong can be an instrument for even practicing Bhakti and Karma Yoga.

Kundalini Yoga and the Gong

The most popular style of yoga associated with the gong is Kundalini Yoga as taught by Yogi Bhajan. In fact, without Yogi Bhajan and Kundalini Yoga, it is unlikely that the development of Gong Yoga would have occurred.

The gong was integrated into Kundalini Yoga classes by the early 1970s, primarily as a way to rebuild the nervous systems of the drug culture hippies recently turned yoga students. Yogi Bhajan often played the gong during meditations at the end of class and also taught several yoga sets in which the gong was played during the exercises and relaxation. His instruction to the dozens of Kundalini ashrams that emerged worldwide in the 1970s and 1980s was to have an ashram gong that could be played to heal all who came to the classes.

Although there are a limited number of Kundalini kriyas (yoga sets) that explicitly specify playing the gong, the gong can be used in a Kundalini class in much the same way that Kundalini music is played during the class, as a way to focus the mind, raise the vibrations and connect the students to the Naad, or universal sound current.

In many ways, Kundalini Yoga is the most welcoming style of yoga in which to play the gong as classes tend to be done in a meditative sequence with the eyes often closed, using floor postures instead of standing postures. In addition, the teacher does not leave the front of the classroom to make adjustments or give extensive physical demonstrations, but holds the space through verbal instructions and so remains within easy access to the gong.

Sound is used extensively in Kundalini classes, through mantras, songs, and live music, so students are comfortable integrating the gong into their yoga practice. Beginning and intermediate students often comment that practicing breath of fire, the signature pranayama of Kundalini Yoga, is much easier when the gong is played as it helps maintain a steady rhythm of the inhale and exhale.

Other classical Kundalini Yoga practices, such as Sat Kriya, Kirtan Kriya (Sa Ta Na Ma), and Morning Call (Ek Ong Kar mantra), lend themselves well to practice with the gong.

Sat Kriya

How to Do It: Sitting on the heels, raise the arms above the head and interlace the fingers and cross the thumbs. Extend both index fingers together in the air above the crown of the head. Breathe as needed to chant the mantra SAT NAM (in this case, the sound *sat* rhymes with "but" and *nam* rhymes with "mom"). On the sound SAT, contract the navel point and project the sound. On the sound NAM, relax the contraction and let the sound escape from the third eye, connecting the third chakra to the sixth chakra. Chant at the rate of 8 times per ten seconds. After 3 minutes, inhale and apply the root lock, mulabandha, and then relax with the exhale.

Playing the Gong: The gong is struck below the center area on SAT firmly and with a lighter strike below the top rim on NAM, playing the gong in the areas of the third and sixth chakra. At the end on the inhale, let the sound of the gong naturally decay as the energy is pulled up with the root lock.

Sat Kriya

Kirtan Kriya (Sa Ta Na Ma Meditation)

How to Do It: Sitting in a meditative pose, chant the four sounds of SA TA NA MA out loud as the thumb is touched successively to the index finger (SA), middle finger (TA), ring finger (NA), and little finger (MA). Each repetition takes about 5 seconds. After 2 minutes chanting out loud, continue with a whispered sound for 2 more minutes. Then repeat the mantra silently for 4 minutes as you continue to touch the thumb to the four fingers with the silent sounds. Return to a whispered chant for 2 more minutes, and then finally chant out loud for the last 2 minutes. At the end, inhale and stretch the arms over the head, twist to the left, twist to the right, and then exhale to the center. Inhale again with arms still over the head and shake the arms and hands. Exhale and keep shaking. Inhale and keep shaking and then exhale the arms and hands down.

Playing the Gong: The gong is struck for each sound made, either out loud, whispered or silent. The gong is played consistently in a four-part sequence, over the four major percussion points 9-12-3-6.

The sequence can be played at a medium volume when chanting out loud, then medium to soft volume when whispered, and softly when chanted silently.

Long Ek Ong Kar Sat Nam Siri Wahe Guru Meditation

How to Do It: Sit in a meditative posture with the thumb touching the index finger tips in gyan mudra and close the eyes. Inhale and chant the sound EK from the base of the spine (root chakra) in a short projective burst, using about 10% of the breath. On the same breath, vibrate the sound ONG at the pelvic area (second chakra) for half of the remaining of the breath, then finish the remaining breath by chanting the sound KAR at the navel point (third chakra). Inhale a deep second breath and chant the sound SAT in a short and strong way at the heart (fourth chakra) and use almost all the rest of the breath in the extended sound NAM at the throat (fifth chakra), saving a small mount of breath for the sound SIRI chanted at the brow point (sixth chakra). Take a half breath inhale and chant the sound WAHE at the top of the head (seventh chakra) and let the final sound GURU be released into the aura around the body (eighth chakra). The full chant takes approximately 40 to 45 seconds. Repeat the full chant for 7 minutes or more as desired. Then inhale and apply the root lock, mulabandha, pull the energy up through the chakras and then relax with the exhale.

Playing the Gong: The gong is struck at each of the seven chakra points along the vertical axis of the gong, beginning above the bottom rim with the sound EK and working up to below the top rim with sound WAHE. With the sound GURU, the gong can be played around the rim or simply allowed to decay after the seventh strike. It may be necessary to muffle or still the gong after the first breath is exhausted (after KAR is chanted), again after the second breath (after SIRI is chanted), and finally at the end (after GURU is chanted) to create a pause the next repetition of the chant.

Hatha Yoga and the Gong

A popular style of yoga in the Western world is Hatha Yoga, a system associated with the practice of asanas or postures. Because of the need to demonstrate and occasionally assist with the postures, it is often necessary to have a gong player as a dedicated accompanist so the teacher can be free to direct the performance of the asanas.

Ideally the gong player is also a Hatha teacher or an experienced practitioner so they can anticipate the energetic effects of the various postures as well as the sequencing needs of the teacher.

The gong can be very effective in a Hatha class when postures are held for several breaths, freeing the teacher to play the gong and use the sound to focus the student's attention.

The other consideration in using the gong in a Hatha class is to strike the right balance between giving enough space for the teacher to instruct and guide and using the gong effectively. It may be necessary to muffle or silence the gong often when using it in a Hatha class.

Vinyasa Flow Yoga and the Gong

Playing the gong with the Vinyasa Flow styles of yoga, which consist of repeated movements and asana sequences connected with the breath, bring both opportunities and challenges in the teaching of Gong Yoga.

The challenge of playing the gong in the Vinyasa Flow environment is to match the rhythm of the gong with the flow of the practice. The gong must seem to ride on the breath of the practitioners, neither hurrying nor delaying the flow of the postures that arise from an inherent rhythm that is guided by the teacher's instructions and the collective movement of the students. Without this subtle attunement of the playing rhythm of the gong to the flow of the practice, the sound becomes intrusive and frustrating. To be able to play the gong effectively for this style of yoga, one must be an accomplished practitioner as well.

The opportunity of using the gong is Vinyasa Flow yoga classes is the ability to create a flowing rhythm that is maintained by the gong, thus freeing both student and the teacher from directing and attempting to create the group conscious and movement that makes up a flow practice.

The gong can be used to signal a vinyasa or transition from one posture to the next with a strike. Also, the gong can be used as the timer for holding one posture and from moving into the next asana.

Ashtanga Yoga and the Gong

The Ashtanga style of yoga popularized by Pattabhi Jois presents special opportunities for the Gong Yoga teacher with its consistent regimen of postures that are repeated over six series.

Because each Ashtanga class follows a format of invariable sequences, students learn the series of postures over time and can become independent of following the teacher's directions. There is less need for the teacher to talk students through the postures and that frees space for both the teachers and the students to go deeper into the sound of the gong when it is played in class. On the other hand, the Ashtanga teacher spends much time with the demonstration of postures and making adjustments. Because of the student-intensive nature of the practice, Ashtanga teachers will benefit by having a separate gong player for the class.

Another use for the gong in Ashtanga Yoga is as a counter for the five breaths that most postures require. A consideration, however, is that many times the group breathing of the class, in which the breath is heard, serves as personal soundtrack for the movement that might be diluted by the sound of the gong.

One contraindication for the Ashtanga practice while using the gong is that the gong should not be played while the student (or the teacher!) is in headstand, a posture that is often held for 25 breaths in the Ashtanga finishing sequence. The effect of the gong on the crown chakra is profound and its sound can be overly activating and disturbing for an extended headstand practice.

On the other hand, the last posture of the Ashtanga finishing series, Tolasana (or Utpluthi), in which the body is lifted off the ground and supported on the arms and hands while in Lotus pose, is one of the best asanas in the series to play the gong, usually in a fast and moderately loud volume to create a climatic upward surge of energy at the end of the class and before relaxation.

Restorative Yoga and the Gong

Restorative Yoga uses blankets, blocks, bolsters and other props to provide support to hold passive postures for an extended length of time. This static and relaxing approach to yoga is a natural application for the gong.

When postures can be held for three minutes or more, the sound of the gong can deepen the experience and create great release. When feasible, holding a single restorative posture for eleven minutes while the gong is played can give optimum benefits as the glandular system is completely rebalanced.

Perhaps the three best restorative poses for a gong relaxation are Supported Child Pose, Supported Hip Openers, and Supported Heart Opener. These poses work on different chakras and organs and can also be done at the end of any regular yoga class as well as being part of a Restorative Yoga class.

Supported Child Pose (Salamba Balasana)

How to Do It: Sitting on the heels, fold forward over a stack of folded blankets or a bolster so the head and chest are supported off the floor. Turn the head so the neck is comfortable. Relax for 3 to 5 minutes in this position, and allow the breath to move deeply into the body.

Playing the Gong: Like many restorative poses, the gong is played softly and slowly, with downward strokes on the bottom half of the gong. Let the gong match or guide the breath to 4 to 8 strikes or breaths per minute, allowing the sound to be regular and monotonic. After 3 minutes, let the gong become softer and softer for the last 1-2 minutes of the posture.

Supported Heart Opener (Supta Anahata Chakra)

How to Do It: Lying on the floor, place folded blankets or a bolster under the knees to support the hips. Place a rolled blanket below the shoulders so the heart is lifted and another rolled blanket under the neck to support the head. Let the arms fall open above your shoulders, elbows comfortable bent. Relax for 3 to 5 minutes in this position, and allow the breath to move through the heart.

Playing the Gong: The gong is played with a heartbeat rhythm around the center. The rhythm remains steady, with a single beat followed by a double-beat to approximate the heart sound. After 3 minutes of medium soft playing, the volume and strikes can increase for one minute and then soften for the final minute.

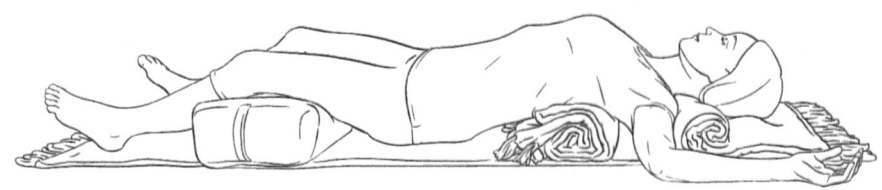

Supported Hip Openers (Supta Baddha Konasana)

How to Do It: Sitting on the floor, bring the soles of the feet together and let the knees fall open to the sides. Place folded blankets or blocks under the knees to support the hips. Place a bolster under the back if you desire and slowly lower the back to the floor. Let the arms fall open to the sides. Relax for 3 to 5 minutes in this position, and allow the breath to move across the hips and pelvic area.

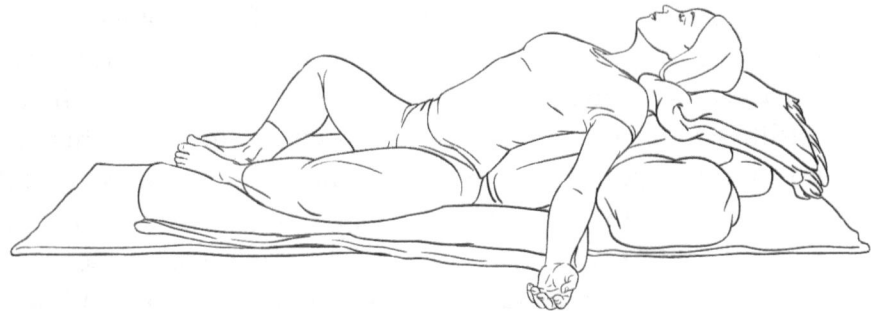

Playing the Gong: The gong is played in a soft and watery manner in the lower third of the gong between the center and the rim. This playing area affects the second chakra. After 3 minutes of medium soft playing, the volume and strikes can increase for one minute and then soften for the final minute.

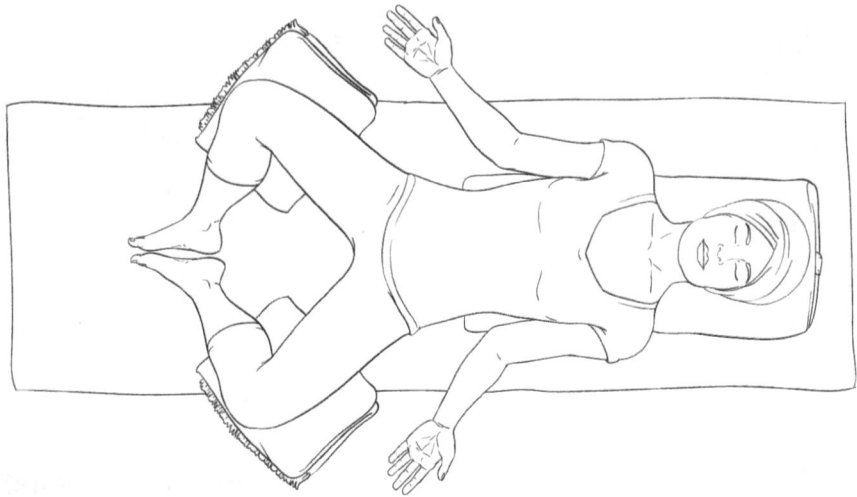

Prenatal Yoga and the Gong

Playing the gong in prenatal yoga classes can be relaxing for mothers-to-be and enjoyable for the babies. Many mothers feel positive movement of their babies in response to a gong well-played.

While the commonly expressed concern for using the gong in a prenatal yoga class is to avoid playing it so that it disturbs the baby, in reality the rule is to not play the gong loudly or aggressively in such a manner that creates anxiety or fear in the mother. For the most part, the baby in the amniotic fluid of the mother experiences the sound of the gong in a softly filtered way, like hearing the gong played under water, and responds positively. However, the baby is sensitive to the emotional state and reactions of the mother and will not enjoy the gong if the mother is experiencing anxiety around it.

The mother's sensitivity to the gong increases in the last trimester, and it can bring up fears if played loudly or aggressively. In such cases, the gong should be played in a soft and soothing manner. One specialized use of the gong during the last trimester is to bring the baby into a better birthing position. Some midwives have even used the gong to turn or spin a baby who is breeched.

This can be done by playing the gong in a manner that brings deep relaxation while holding one or more of these yoga asanas described here.

Uttana Shishosana (Extended Puppy Pose)

Also known in Yin Yoga as Anahatasana (Heart-melting Pose)

This yoga posture appears to be a cross between Child's Pose (Balasana) and Downward Dog (Adho Mukha Svanasana) and has many health benefits, including helping with flexibility of the spine and relieving the symptoms of chronic stress and insomnia. It is also an excellent position to create the proper alignment of the baby before delivery, or to turn or spin the baby.

How To Do It: Come onto the hands and knees, shoulders over wrists and hips over knees with the arms should width apart. Extend the arms out on the floor, reaching away from you, palms down, as you bring your forehead to the floor. The hips stay up in the air, above the knees, with the thighs approximately perpendicular to the floor. If there is tightness, you can place a bolster or cushion under the forehead and bring the arms closer back to the body. Hold the posture for up to one minute, or up to three minutes if comfortable.

Playing the Gong: The gong is played on the bottom half with soft downward strokes at a slow and regular pace.

Bitilasana (Cow Pose)

This yoga posture is often paired with the Cat Pose (Marjariasana) to perform Cat-Cow movement. Cow has several health benefits, including releasing tension in the low back and regulating the thyroid gland. It is also an excellent position to create the proper tilt of the hips before delivery, or to turn or spin the baby.

How To Do It: Come onto the hands and knees, shoulders over wrists and hips over knees with the arms should width apart. Allow the belly to sink toward the floor and lift you head to look straight ahead. Close your eyes. Hold the posture with easy long breathing for up to one minute, or up to three minutes if comfortable.

Playing the Gong: The gong is played on the bottom half with firm downward strokes at a regular pace.

Vasti Udayana (Pelvic Lift)

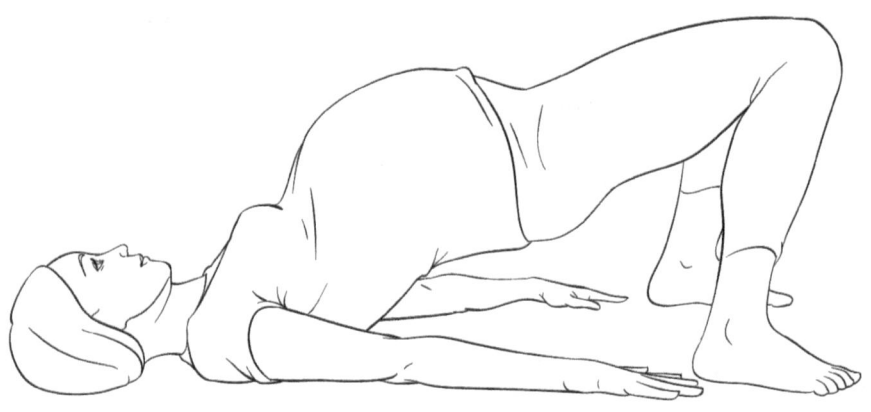

This yoga posture is used therapeutically to strengthen the back and is an excellent pelvic opener that provides the benefits of a backbend. This can be a strenuous prenatal pose and should not be held for long periods of time. It is an excellent strengthener to prepare for delivery and is another position to create the proper tilt of the hips before delivery, or to turn or spin the baby.

How To Do It: Come onto the back and bend the knees so the feet are flat in the floor in front of the hips. Place the arm palms down beside the body. As you inhale, press the hips off the floor, using the feet, legs, hands and arms. As you exhale, slowly lower the hips back to the floor. Repeat several times as comfortable.

Playing the Gong: The gong is played on the top half with a short upward strike when inhaling and on the bottom half with a short downward strike when exhaling. After the hips relax down, the gong is played softly for a minute.

Children's Yoga and the Gong

Playing the gong for a children's yoga class has special requirements depending upon the age group. For children over the age of 12, the gong can generally be played as for adult yoga students. The gong does affect the glandular system so after children enter puberty, the gong can be a welcome balancing influence on the pituitary and pineal glands. Children of this age can enjoy a gong relaxation for up to 10 minutes with good benefit. Extended gong playing may produce anxiety in some children and can be too challenging for their nervous systems.

For younger children, the gong should be introduced as a musical instrument by demonstrating how the various sounds are produced, and even inviting them to gently strike the gong to create a relationship with it. They may wish to sit with their eyes open as the gong is played instead of closing the eyes or lying down. In some cases, they can hold a simple yoga pose while the gong is played almost like a soundtrack.

Excellent results have been obtained with special needs children by using the gong in yoga classes. Autistic children are especially attracted to the gong when they are allowed to play it, although care must be taken to not play the gong overly loud for them.

Children with attention deficient disorders can learn to focus better when the gong is played in postures or short meditations. While it is no surprise that the gong has been successfully used in yoga classes for blind children, deaf children are also fascinated by the gong and benefit from the vibration that is transmitted through the floor and around the room.

Yoga for Seniors and the Gong

Playing the gong for seniors and populations who may be chair-bound has special rewards. The special consideration for a Gong Yoga class for seniors is to make sure that the students do not have their hearing aids on when the gong is played. Have them turn the hearing aid completely off or remove it before the gong is played. Amplification of the gong through hearing aids can create pain and possible injury.

The gong should be played slowly and softly for people over the age of 75. The idea is to soothe and not challenge the listener or to create anxiety with overly loud sounds.

An easy and enjoyable yoga exercise using the gong for seniors is to have them imagine the sound like the waves of the ocean and to allow their breath to move up and down with the sound. If movement is desired, the students can move their hands and arms slowly up and down in rhythm with the gong while sitting in a chair.

Guidelines for Teaching Gong Yoga

Depending upon the class structure and the playing skill of the teacher, the teacher can both instruct the class as well as play the gong. This works well with relaxation and meditation when the students need little guidance from the teacher.

On the other hand, if the teacher needs to actively guide the students through an asana practice or otherwise be fully engaged in instruction, then a second person may be needed to play the gong. Such an arrangement requires a good rapport between the teacher and gong player so as to strike an appropriate balance between spoken instruction and the playing of the gong. The gong should be played at a very low level, if at all, if the teacher needs to speak or interact with the students. At the same time, the teacher needs to be sensitive when it is better to remain silent and let the gong do its work.

The gong player should always be in a subservient role to the teacher, neither speaking nor instructing the students, once the class has begun. In addition the gong player needs to be tuned in to the changing needs of the class as it unfolds and be ready to quickly support the teacher. Each yoga class develops a rhythm of its own according to the students and energy in the room, and the gong player must be open to change and accommodation.

Regardless if the teacher plays the gong or is assisted by a gong player, the class needs to be orchestrated to maximize the impact of the sound of the gong. There should be sufficient listening space as the gong is interweaved into the class experience. Realize that the gong is never simply background music. It creates a dominant undertone and audible presence that moves and changes energy from moment to moment, breath to breath.

Teaching and Playing the Gong

Here are some helpful guidelines when teaching Gong Yoga:

- Do not give complicated verbal instructions to the students while the gong is played. While it is better to not speak at all while the gong is playing, realize you will have to project loudly if you must say something vital.

- Do not over orchestrate the class with multiple gong sessions. Playing the gong a few times will often be sufficient.

- Let students know when you are about to play the gong if they do not already expect it.

- If some students in class have never heard the gong before, prepare them for the experience with instructions to relax into the sound and use the breath to allow the experience to be received. Perhaps even have them watch you strike the gong the first time so they can see the sound being made.

- Be cognizant that some people may react negatively to the sound of the gong the first time they hear it, particularly if they have issues around trust, letting go, tightly held boundaries, or a history of unpleasant associations with loud or unusual sounds. On the other hand, these same people can develop a healthy and appreciative relationship with the gong once it begins to clear out feelings of anxiety and old traumas.

- Be aware that whenever the gong is played, it will open and change energy. People may process emotional clearing from the gong as they continue through the rest of the class and this may color the experience of the remainder of the class.

- Bring people out of the gong space gently, with the soothing sound of your voice or a period of silence. Do not rush the transition from listening to the gong to actively doing a yoga posture as there can be a disassociation from the physical body when listening to the gong.

Gong Maps and Playing Techniques

These gong maps can help refine your playing techniques and are based upon the premise that different playing areas of the gong produce different effects in the listener. These effects can be implemented in all the methods of yoga: asanas, pranayama, meditation and relaxation.

The Top and Bottom Areas of the Gong

Imagine a horizontal line across the face of the gong connecting percussion point 9 to percussion point 3 that divides the gong into an upper horizontal half and a bottom horizontal half. Each of these areas can be played to create different effects as shown in the map.

The Side Areas of the Gong

Imagine a vertical line down the center of the gong connecting percussion point 12 to percussion point 6 that divides the gong into an right vertical half and a left vertical half. Notice that while the top and bottom areas are the same for all players, the side nearest the player (inside) is the right vertical area of the gong if the player is right-handed and the left side of the gong if the player is left handed. Each area can be played to create the effects as shown in the map.

The Four Energy Areas

Finally, the gong can be divided by a horizontal axis that bisects the center of the gong and a vertical axis from top to bottom.

The resulting quadrants the two intersecting axis produce create four energy areas that can be played to achieve certain effects in a yoga practice, such as either to energize or to relax, or to elevate or to ground. Intuitively, the upper half of the gong elevates, the bottom half grounds, the far side of the gong projects and the inner side of the gong receives. The map of the four energy areas is for the right-handed player and is mirrored for left handed players.

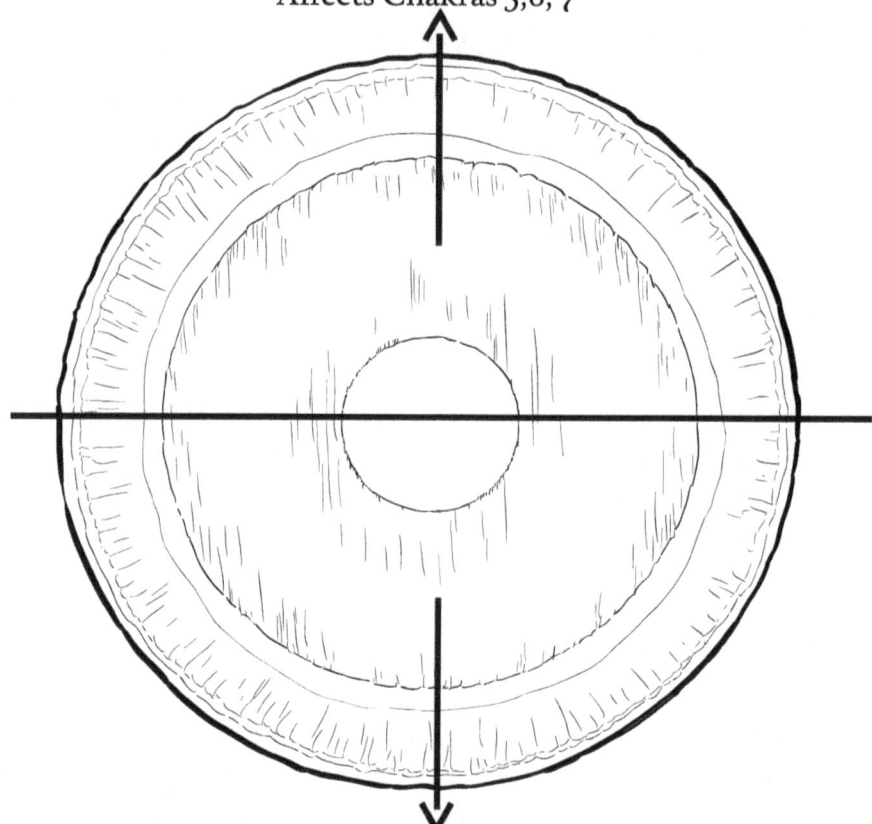

Playing the Far Area of the Gong
(the area away from player)
Creates Projective Energy
Affects the Analytical Body
Stimulates Pingala Nadi
Increases Brimhana
Supports Outward Moving Postures
Affects Sympathetic Nervous System

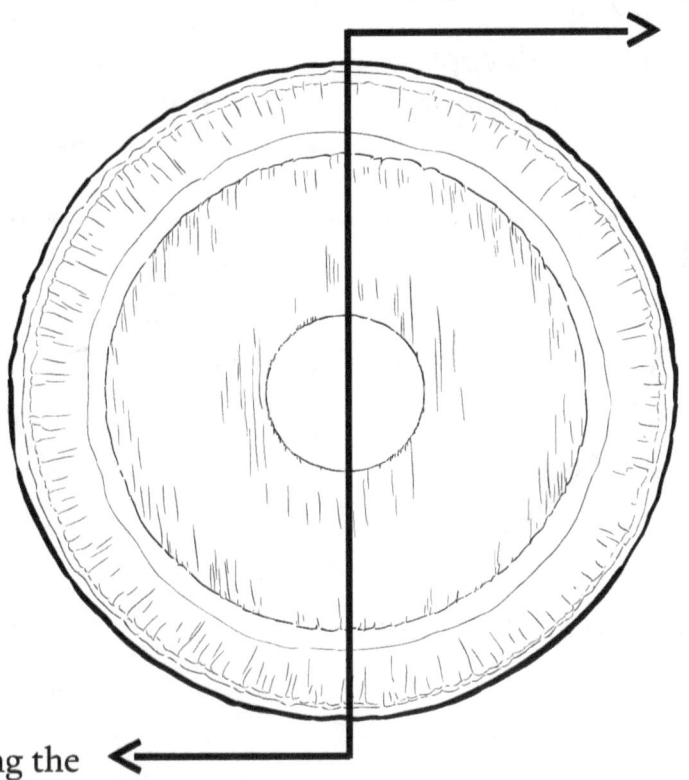

Playing the
Inner Area of the Gong
(the area next to player)
Creates Receptive Energy
Affects the Intuitive Body
Stimulates Ida Nadi
Increases Langhana
Supports Inward Moving Postures
Affects Parasympathetic System

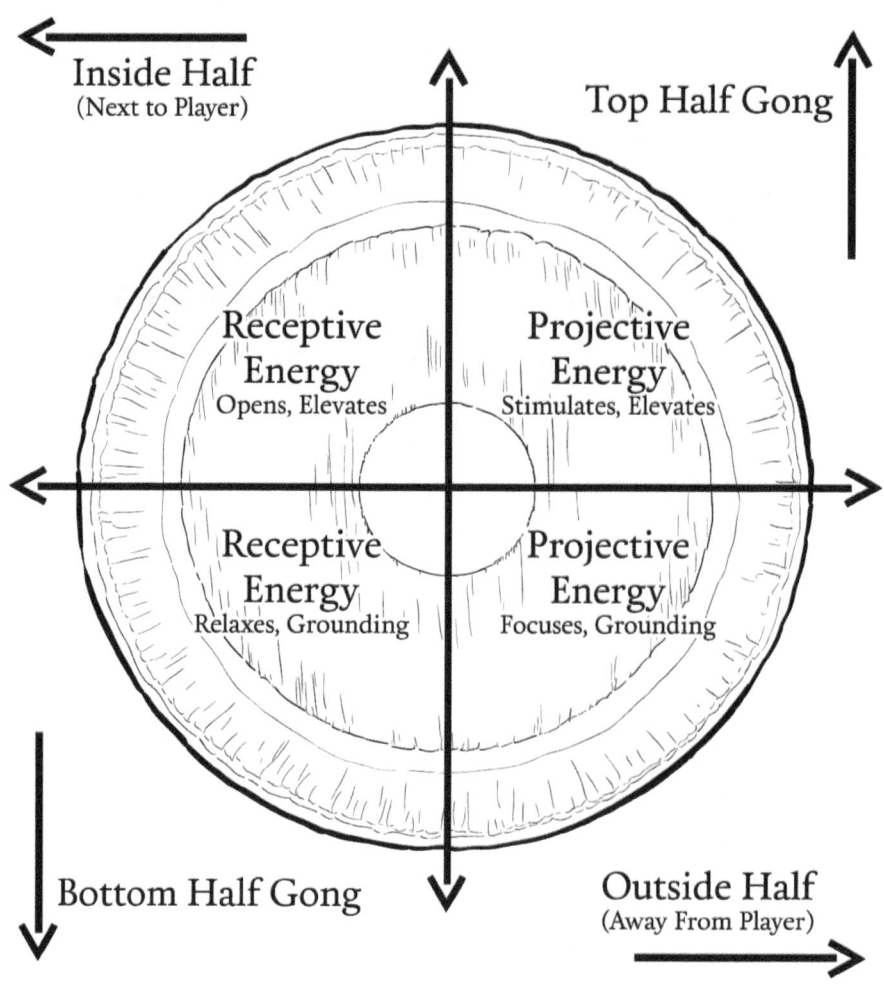

The Structure of a Gong Yoga Class

There is a difference between playing the gong in your yoga class and teaching a Gong Yoga class, and there is a structure that distinguishes the practice, as follows:

- Gong Opening
- Gong Pranayama
- Gong Kriya
- Gong Meditation
- Gong Relaxation
- Gong Closing

There are many variations within this structure that can be adapted to all styles of yoga.

Gong Opening: Beginning a Gong Yoga Class

Begin the class with a centering mantra. This should be done silently for yourself as the player.

Remain in silence as you strike the gong slowly three times near the center of the gong. Allow the sound to decay between the strikes and fill the room with its sound. After the third strike, remain in silence for as long as the previous strikes took. These three strikes, and the resulting silence, introduce the sound of the gong and correspond to the trinity field concept of consciousness in the practice of yoga.

The first strike represents the waking state of mental consciousness and the gross form of the universe that is contained in the anamaya kosha and the Physical Body (*Sthula Sharira*).

The second strike represents the dreaming state of the active unconscious processing level of the mind and the subtle realm of the universe that is contained in the pranamaya kosha, manamaya kosha, vijnanamaya kosha and the Subtle Body (*Sukshma Sharira*).

The third strike represents the deep sleep state of the mind and its subconscious aspects where the *samskaras*, or impetus for karma arises and the causal realm of the universe that is contained in the anandamaya kosha and the Causal Body (*Karana Sharira*).

The silence that follows the three strikes represents the state known as *Turiya*, or infinite consciousness where the three levels of mind and being are transcended.

After the silence, you can now introduce the class, or you can chant a mantra with the class according to your yoga tradition. For example, a Kundalini Yoga teacher would chant *Ong Namo Guru Dev Namo* three times while an Ashtanga teacher would use the invocation beginning with *Vande Gurunam Charanaravinde*.

After the group chanting ends, the gong can be struck a single time to mark the beginning of formal instruction, or a simply conscious inhale and exhale may be done.

Gong Pranayama: Connecting Sound to Energy

Since the gong works powerfully with moving prana through the body, it is helpful to begin the class with a gong pranayama practice to initiate the flow of breath. This could be a Breath of Fire practice with the gong if you are a Kundalini Yoga teacher, alternate nostril breathing if you are a Hatha teacher, Ujiya breath if you are an Ashtanga teacher, or simple long deep breathing, using the gong to regulate the inhale and exhale.

Gong Kriya: Using Sound With Movement

A kriya is a sequence of asanas, pranayamas, mudras, bandhas, and mantra that create a state of meditation. Some traditions, such as Kundalini and Ashtanga Yoga, have formalized kriyas that are strictly followed by the teachers. While some Hatha styles in the Western world have specific sequences or kriyas they follow in accordance with their tradition, there is often the possibility to create one's own sequence. Regardless of the yoga style or tradition, the kriya in a Gong Yoga class has a specific purpose (such as working on a chakra, an organ, or psychological state) in addition to preparing the practitioner for meditation.

Within this kriya, the teacher can take the opportunity to play the gong with one or more asanas or exercises. A reasonable rule is to play the gong one to three times during the class. For some kriyas, and if appropriate for the specific exercises and class flow, the gong can be played more, following the guidelines already given.

Gong Meditation: Taking the Sound Within

Following the kriya, the Gong Yoga class can lead directly into a gong relaxation and the meditation may be omitted. If a formal meditation is desired, then it may be done before the relaxation.

A meditation should last for a minimum of 3 minutes, although a 7-minute threshold is usually required for the sound of the gong to deeply affect the nervous system and mind. An 11-minute meditation is ideal for experienced students. For advanced practices and workshops, the meditation can be extended to 31-minutes.

Gong Relaxation: Integration and Clearing

If a gong meditation was used, then the relaxation afterwards can be done in silence, at least for a few minutes. Otherwise, the gong may be played as part of the relaxation for a minimum of 7 minutes to fully activate the parasympathetic nervous system. Be aware that a gong relaxation longer than 15 minutes at the end of the class may overwhelm the effects of the kriya and meditation, or change the sattvic state of relaxation into a tamasic nap. At the end of the gong relaxation, there should be a minute of silence before speaking and bringing the students out of relaxation.

Gong Closing: Ending a Gong Yoga Class

The Gong Yoga class may be closed with a mantra, a song, or a blessing. Depending upon the tradition and the energy of the class, the gong can also be struck to signal the closing of the sacred space.

Sat Nam

Gong Therapy

Sound Healing and Yoga

Mehtab Benton

Gong Therapy: Sound Healing and Yoga is a comprehensive book on using the gong and the practices of yoga to create a therapeutic environment and transformational experience for physical, mental and spiritual excellence.

Written for sound healers, yoga teachers, gong players, and therapists, this book gives you the tools and information to conduct one-on-one private sessions as well as guidelines for using the gong as a therapeutic instrument in a group setting.

Gong Therapy: Sound Healing and Yoga includes these topics:

- The Basis of Sound Healing and Yoga Therapy
- How to Structure a Gong Therapy Session
- How to Play the Gong Therapeutically
- Preparing the Gong Therapy Environment
- Client Assessment and Development of a Therapy Session
- Considerations for Selecting and Using Gongs
- Using Mudras, Mantras, and Pranayamas Therapeutically
- Guided Meditation and Relaxation for Gong Therapy
- Gong Therapy for Groups
- Using Gong Therapy with Other Healing Modalities
- Gong Therapy as a Profession

Mehtab Benton has trained hundreds of gong players and yoga teachers worldwide. He is the originator and author of *Gong Yoga: Healing and Enlightenment Through Sound,* published in five international editions and translations. His DVD course *How To Play the Gong* is a best-selling video for beginners. A practitioner and teacher of Kundalini Yoga for over 40 years, Mehtab has an educational background in psychology and yoga therapy and is a certified Vedic Astrologer.

www.bookshelfpress.com

How to Play the Gong

DVD Training Course

Mehtab Benton

How to Play the Gong is the complete video instructional course for self-study and mastery of the gong.

Performed and written by Mehtab Benton, author of GONG YOGA, this two-volume DVD course demonstrates both basic and advanced playing techniques through a series of practice sessions.

Volume 1 introduces you to the different playing areas of the gong, specific percussion points, and working with the mallet strikes to control volume and create rhythms.

Volume 2 begins with using combination strokes to create a rich wall of sound and then building into more intricate sequences. You'll learn how to use multiple mallets and several gongs to create an extended sound session through intuitive playing. *Bonus features* include using the gong with the chakras and a live outdoor performance.

Playing the gong does not require any prior musical experience. You begin with the basic mallet strokes, learn playing sequences and then create your own gong sessions for relaxation, meditation, and healing.

Mehtab Benton is the author of *Gong Yoga: Healing and Enlightenment Through Sound*, and the master teacher of the video course *How to Play the Gong*. He has trained hundreds of yoga teachers and therapists in the art and science of playing the gong. He is an Integrative Yoga Therapist and yoga teacher trainer with a background in counseling and psychology.

Available from Bookshelf Press
www.bookshelfpress.com

Gong Yoga

Healing and Enlightenment Through Sound

Mehtab Benton

Gong Yoga is the first comprehensive book on practicing and teaching yoga with the sound of the gong. You will learn about the origin, history and use of the gong for yoga and meditation as well as its current therapeutic applications for healing and transformation.

The book contains a step-by-step training guide to teach you how to play the gong through a series of practice sessions. You will learn the basic techniques to play the gong as well as advanced techniques to create your own gong playing sessions. You will learn how to structure gong yoga classes and gong yoga therapy sessions for your students and clients.

A comprehensive chapter on Yoga and the Gong describes the chakras, the major energy channels of the body (the nadis), and the five sheaths of existence (the koshas), that are key to understanding how the gong integrates with the practice of yoga. Special sections explain the use of Kundalini Yoga mantras for playing the gong, how to select and care for your gong and additional resources to develop your skills.

Written by a long-time yoga teacher and international trainer of students and therapists in the art of playing the gong for meditation and healing.

"Information on how to play the gong and the spiritual aspects of the sound of the gong are difficult to find. **GONG YOGA** *is a wonderful introduction to all aspects of the gong and the yoga that is associated with it. The interesting history of the gong, its uses in Western and Eastern music, how to play it and the gong's effects on the body's energetic system are all discussed. FIVE STARS!"*

Available from Bookshelf Press and all major booksellers
www.bookshelfpress.com

Astrology Yoga

Cosmic Cycles of Transformation

Mehtab Benton

Astrology Yoga is the first comprehensive book on the practice of Yoga using the ancient science of Vedic Astrology, or Jyotish.

Written for yoga practitioners with a limited knowledge of astrology, this book explains the dynamic and vital relationship that has always existed between these two ancient Vedic sciences and how you can use this knowledge to accelerate your transformation by working with your personal planetary energies.

You will learn about your yogic Sun sign and Moon sign, the specific karmic issues in your life, the most appropriate yoga practices based on your birth date, and the most beneficial times to do your yoga practices over the day, during the week, and throughout all the cycles of your life. The book describes the original relationship between Eastern or Vedic astrology and yoga and the differences between Yoga astrology and western astrology. You'll learn about the nine major planetary energies, the twelve signs, and the twelve life areas of astrology yoga.

You will learn about your own astrological life cycles that affect your consciousness and yoga practices, as well as the universal cosmic cycles that affect everyone. Yoga practices for moon phases, days of the week, months of the year, and hours of the day, as well as for special occasions of the solstices, equinoxes and eclipses, are discussed to help you design a yoga practice that supports you through each cycle of your life.

Written by a life-long practitioner and teacher of Yoga as well as a certified Vedic astrologer, Astrology Yoga provides you with a personal roadmap for your journey to enlightenment.

Available from Bookshelf Press and all major booksellers
www.bookshelfpress.com

About Bookshelf Press

Bookshelf Press is a print and electronic publisher of books on yoga, health, Eastern astrology, and literary works of high imagination.

Bookshelf Press retains all subsidiary rights for its books. Rights are available through the publisher for foreign editions and other media adaptations.

Wholesale and retail orders are available directly from the publisher.

www.bookshelfpress.com

www.ingramcontent.com/pod-product-compliance
Lightning Source LLC
Chambersburg PA
CBHW052100280426
43673CB00070B/34